THE
EX-GIRLFRIEND
OF MY
EX-GIRLFRIEND
IS MY
GIRLFRIEND

THE EX-GIRLFRIEND OF MY EX-GIRLFRIEND IS MY GIRLFRIEND

Advice on Queer Dating, Love, and Friendship

WRITTEN BY
Maddy Court

ILLUSTRATED BY
Kelsey Wroten

CHRONICLE BOOKS
SAN FRANCISCO

Library of Congress Cataloging-in-Publication Data

Names: Court, Maddy, author. | Wroten, Kelsey, illustrator.
Title: The ex-girlfriend of my ex-girlfriend is my girlfriend : advice on queer dating, love, and friendship / written by Maddy Court ; illustrated by Kelsey Wroten.
Description: San Francisco : Chronicle Books, [2021].
Identifiers: LCCN 2020046747 | ISBN 9781797201825
Subjects: LCSH: Lesbians—Life skills guides. | Sexual minorities—Life skills guides. | Lesbianism. | Dating (Social customs) | Sex counseling.
Classification: LCC HQ75.5 .C68 2021 | DDC 306.76—dc23
LC record available at https://lccn.loc.gov/2020046747

Manufactured in China.

MIX
Paper from
responsible sources
FSC™ C008047
www.fsc.org

Design by Lizzie Vaughan.

10 9 8 7 6 5 4 3 2

Chronicle books and gifts are available at special quantity discounts to corporations, professional associations, literacy programs, and other organizations. For details and discount information, please contact our premiums department at corporatesales@chroniclebooks.com or at 1-800-759-0190.

Chronicle Books LLC
680 Second Street
San Francisco, California 94107
www.chroniclebooks.com

This book is dedicated to everyone who
has ever Googled the words *am I gay?*

CONTENTS

INTRODUCTION

Dear Readers,

This is a book about queer love and relationships. I wrote it entirely in bed. I tried, repeatedly, to find a respectable writing place like a coffee shop, library, or the food court of an abandoned mall. But I always ended up back in bed, braless and snacking. Even though I'm a lesbian, writing about emotions and relationships is exhausting for me. I hate feeling like an authority figure or like I'm telling other people what to do. I'm not a therapist or a mental health professional. The fact that I'm writing an introduction to a book still feels implausible to me, like a dream.

The Ex-Girlfriend of My Ex-Girlfriend Is My Girlfriend began as a zine—a black-and-white booklet that I wrote, copied, folded, and stapled together all by myself. At the time, I was twenty-five and languishing in a women's studies grad program. I was bitingly lonely. I spent my days writing long, airless essays about feminism that nobody, not even my professors, wanted to read. I presented my work at a conference and there were three people in the audience, including my mom. On top of everything, I was flat broke. I could barely afford my rent, let alone the minimum payment on my Discover card. One night, I took a bath and evaluated my resources. I had free university printing and a few thousand followers on Instagram. As a lesbian on the internet, I was constantly getting DMs from strangers seeking advice—messages like, "I think I'm gay?" or "Should my girlfriend and I open our relationship?" All the ingredients for a zine about queer dating, friendship, and love were right there in front of me.

I expected to sell fifty copies of The Ex-Girlfriend of My Ex-Girlfriend Is My Girlfriend, maybe a hundred. I received four hundred orders the first week alone. Readers shared the zine and told their friends. Over the next year, I hired my mom to help with operations and wrote two more volumes—The Ex-Girlfriend of My Ex-Girlfriend Is My Wife and The Ex-Girlfriend of My Ex-Girlfriend Is My

Ex-Wife. Today, there are over ten thousand copies of the *Ex-Girlfriend* zines around the world. The zines are the most humbling, gratifying thing I have ever done. When Kelsey Wroten, my favorite artist and graphic novelist, asked me to collaborate on a full-color book, I was like, YES.

Kelsey is from Kansas. I'm from Wisconsin. We came out at a time when queer books, movies, and other media were scarce. The internet existed but it wasn't the searchable, free-flowing well of queer expression that it is today. When we envisioned this book, we wanted readers to feel seen and validated in a way that we had to wait until college to experience. Our hope was that queers of all stripes would see their relationships, anxieties, and heartbreaks reflected in these pages.

All of the questions in this book are from real people. All names have been changed. We put out an open call for submissions and selected questions that did justice to the range of identities and concerns we saw in the responses. Some of the queries were out of my depth, so Kelsey and I enlisted the help of seven guest experts—JD Samson, Samantha Irby, Lola Pellegrino, Mey Rude, Ellen Kempner, Tyler Ford, and Kalyn Rose Heffernan. In spite of the wide-ranging topics covered in these questions, one book cannot possibly encapsulate every queer experience—not even close. Still, we hope that you see enough of yourself in these letters to know that whatever you're going through, someone out there can relate.

Kelsey and I hope this book is useful to you. When you're done, we hope you pass it along to a friend.

XOXO,
MADDY COURT & KELSEY WROTEN

A NOTE ON LANGUAGE AND CONTENT

While putting this book together, we realized that there is no cohesive or correct language to talk about queer identities and experiences. In the following pages, you might see people reclaim slurs for themselves or otherwise use language that doesn't feel right to you. Because this is a book about the experiences of queer people, there are discussions of homophobia, transphobia, ableism, fatphobia, and other forms of oppression throughout. There is a question about abuse on page 146 and a question about negative body image on page 42.

FIRSTS & THIRSTS

CRUSHES & FIRST DATES

CHAPTER ONE

I was destroyed when my first girlfriend broke up with me. I tried to take a leave of absence from college, just so I wouldn't have to see her walking around campus with her new girlfriend. The only thing that stopped me was meeting with my dean and learning that leaving would mean forfeiting my financial aid. It was a dark time. I remember lying on my extra-long twin bed and just watching the moon through my window. I was like, *So this is what all those songs and poems are about.* I felt like I'd joined a special club for people who had loved and lost. In the decade or so since, I've weathered dozens of breakups. I've felt high levels of disappointment, rejection, and anger. I've cried on city buses in Portland, OR; Philadelphia; Brooklyn; and Madison, WI. Still, I will never be as unmoored or devastated as I was after my first breakup.

When you're in love for the first time, everything is THE MOST. Your love is the most profound. The sex you're having is the BEST. No relationship will ever compare. Not to be a cynical dyke who has walked this earth for a hundred years, but these feelings will pass. They will dissipate like dust in the wind, and you will be free. You will love and date again, and you'll be a wiser, more grounded partner because you've done it all before.

I have two strikes against me. I have been closeted a long time, for one. So far so good on opening up to people, that's great. I think it is fairly obvious at this point that I'm not straight, though I am told "everyone in my hometown" knew I was gay since college. Whatever. But here's the thing. I also have a chronic illness (most likely endo) that makes sex and orgasm often very, very painful. I have been trying to heal this and it's better. But still, what do you think is a good way to approach dates? I have had ladies flirt with me and I am reasonably attractive I guess . . . but I'm so terrified of rejection and talking about this pain issue. Also, I have tried a few times to ask girls out and it was a failure and they had a boyfriend in another country or whatever. Loveless forever, feel my tears of woe.

—LORA, 40

A. A lot of conventional relationship advice will tell you to stop worrying about rejection—getting turned down is an inevitable part of dating and being alive. My friend Logan is a master of casual dating, and her whole philosophy is: "I don't like everyone I meet, so I don't expect everyone to like me." Still, I think it's important to honor how gutting and disheartening rejection can feel—especially when the world has made you feel like your body is wrong or undesirable in some way. My guess is that on a logical level, you don't actually want to date anyone who lies and says they have a boyfriend in another country. But on an emotional level, that "no" still feels like a confirmation of your biggest insecurities.

There's an expectation when you come out—especially if you've struggled with your sexuality for a long time—that the skies will open and queer sex gods will rain love and orgasms down upon you. In reality, coming out can be confusing and lonely. It can happen in phases, or over a long time. It's normal to feel disoriented, or like you have to learn how to date all over again. There's a whole new set of words to describe yourself and your desires. Are you butch or femme? A top or a bottom or a switch? What's a service top and is it different from a control top? You might be encountering a lot of people in open relationships for the first time and wondering if nonmonogamy is for you. Also, the dating pool is really, really small when you're queer. It's so small, it's more like a hot tub. The stereotype that lesbians and queer women date their friends, their ex-girlfriends, their friend's ex-girlfriends, and the ex-girlfriends of their ex-girlfriends is absolutely true in my experience. When you're newly out and still searching for a queer community of your own, it can feel like everyone is in a clique and has been best friends for a hundred years. It doesn't help that there are precious few lesbian bars or social spaces for queer women. If you weren't someone who did online dating before, I cannot overstate how essential dating apps can be. The internet will take the guesswork out of deciphering who's queer and available. You can broadcast what you're looking for and know who's interested outright.

You're worried that your endometriosis will scare away potential partners, but what's the point of being queer if you're still stuck with the same rigid, unimaginative blueprints for what sex looks like? One of the best parts of any fledgling relationship is learning how to fuck each other. Also, there are many, many people who want emotional and physical intimacy without sex. I always feel like a jerk when I suggest therapy because therapy is expensive and so obvious. I'm sure you already know that there are sex therapists, physical therapists, and holistic healers who are experts at helping people with endometriosis and other chronic illnesses. You said you've been

working on healing, but this is me encouraging you to ask for guidance and support from a real, qualified professional and not just from me, a former English major.

So how should you approach dates? After I came out, my love life was marked by extreme highs and lows. I felt everything so intensely. I put undue pressure on myself to be in a relationship because I wanted proof that all the pain and turmoil of coming out had been worth it. I was desperate for a happy ending. Instead, I learned that my friends could be family. I also found a lot of comfort and joy in learning about lesbian history, watching lesbian movies, and commiserating with other dykes. Now is the time to make queer friends and explore your local queer communities. Plus, the more you put yourself out into the big gay world, the more potential dates you'll pull into your orbit. ♥

I'm entering my twenties and have only recently entered the queer dating scene. I'm confident in my attraction to women and lack of attraction to men, but every time I get romantically close to a girl, I find myself losing interest the second I admit to having feelings. I can't tell if this is me being conditioned to only want to be friends with other girls (since I was often "one of the boys" growing up), or if there is a cruel countdown clock on my feelings. The girl I am seeing now is so kind and ideally everything I could ask for, but as soon as I told her how I felt, I began to lose interest in seeing her. This is tragic and I'd love some advice.

—DYLAN, 19

A. I could have written this question when I was nineteen. Throughout my teens and early twenties, I made deep emotional deposits in unavailable women. I developed huge, painful crushes on anyone who lived over a thousand miles away, had a girlfriend, or barely knew I existed. When someone showed genuine interest in me, I pushed them away. I'm not exaggerating when I say that I sometimes felt repulsed or suffocated by romantic attention. I knew my feelings were rooted in my own insecurities—I didn't feel deserving of anyone's attention or care, so when someone did like me, I immediately distrusted them. Like you, I recognized a pattern that I needed to change. Therapy and reading about attachment theory helped a lot. It also helped to take stock of my friendships and acknowledge that I was, in fact, capable of giving and receiving love.

You just spent a lot of time questioning and investigating your sexuality, so I don't need to tell you how confusing and mysterious attraction can be. You can admire your girlfriend, even see her as a role model, without wanting to be in a relationship with her. I've definitely met hot, available women and the logical side my brain is like, *What about her?* But then the emotional part of my brain is like, *Nope!* It can be difficult to know when I genuinely don't feel a romantic connection and when I'm sabotaging myself. The older I get, and the more I understand who I'm attracted to and why, the easier it becomes.

Growing up, you were conditioned to see other girls as friends and only friends. It makes sense that the idea of a relationship with another woman might feel impossible to you. You might also have internalized messages from family, religion, and pop culture at large that it's wrong or shameful to be gay. Most queer people don't grow up seeing our lives and stories depicted in mainstream media. I'm barely a decade older than you, and the only queer representation I had in high school was Alex and Marissa on *The OC* and a DVD of *Milk* that I checked out from the public library. There's been a heartening uptick of queer

movies and TV shows in recent years, but it's still easy to internalize the belief that queer lives and relationships are destined for tragedy. The only solution, I think, is to seek out stories about queer women that feel authentic and useful to you. I recommend Tanya Saracho's TV show *Vida*, Dorothy Allison's novel *Bastard Out of Carolina*, and anything by Desiree Akhavan.

There are so many possible reasons for the disinterest you feel toward your girlfriend. You could be someone who prefers casual relationships, in the same way that some people only want to date if there's a potential for marriage or lifelong commitment. Maybe there are other aspects of your life that need attention—if I drew a Venn diagram of my love life, the times when I wanted a girlfriend the most and the times when I was the least emotionally equipped for a relationship would be a perfect circle. Maybe all of this advice is relevant, maybe only some of it is. If it's any consolation, your first forays into queer dating are supposed to be confusing. All you can do is be patient and kind to yourself and your partners. ♥

It's a tale as old as time: I have a crush on my friend, we are both lesbians, I am afraid of ruining our friendship. There are two things that make this more complicated: My best friend and I jointly formed a friendship with my crush, and I feel like acting on my feelings could put not only my friendship with my crush in jeopardy but also affect our whole group dynamic, which I don't want to do to either my best friend or my crush. The other is that I recently ended a long and intense relationship and swore that I was going to take some time off from relationships to heal and learn from that experience . . . but it's only been a couple of months and I'm head over heels for my friend (and, frankly, I was into her while things were going south with my ex, before we broke up). Given both of these factors, I'd usually just ignore this crush and let it float away to the island where all unrequited crushes live. BUT, Maddy, I'm getting so many vibes that she's into me too! She's made so many comments that are just inviting me to confess my feelings, her behavior can get super flirty (it wasn't until about a month ago!), and we've started texting or calling every day (also did not start that until recently). Also, we recently went on a weeklong road trip together that involved some veeeery intimate moments and we still never made out, so maybe that counts against her liking me? I just don't know what to do—should I admit my feelings (knowing she may not be into me) or let this crush go out to pasture?

—MORGAN, 23

𝔸. Your crush is into you. You know it. I know it. The rural gas station clerk you interacted with for twenty seconds on your road trip knows it. Your best friend probably knows too. I can feel the rain clouds gathering, Morgan. By the time you read this, you and your crush will have already surpassed the bounds of friend-ship and entered into makeout territory.

It's true that dating your crush could shift and destabilize the dynamics of your larger friend group. But it's not helpful to assume your best friend will react negatively, or that you can't communicate and work through problems if they arise. You can't be so afraid of potential conflict that you keep a secret from your best friend, or miss out on an exciting new relationship.

You're also worried because you went through a bad breakup a few months ago and were planning on taking this time to be single. It's so, so important to listen to yourself when you need to be alone. If you're mindful not to use your new relationship as a rebound or a distraction, I think you're fine. Like I said, I'm writing this response knowing full well that you and your crush are already u-hauling. ♥

Q. So, being the (reformed?) messy lesbian that I am, I have had varying romantic encounters in the past with a few of my friends. These days I have a gf, we are monogamous, and it's all good. However, I have a close friend—let's call her Sam—whose friendship with me started off as romantic, until I ultimately friend-zoned her. We mutually(!) agreed that we were better as friends, and we've been platonically close ever since! That was four years ago. This past summer, while VERY drunk, Sam sent me an Instagram video saying that even though we're both in relationships, she's always had feelings for me and still has a huge crush. It was one of those videos that couldn't be replayed, and in the morning she texted me asking what she sent because she had blacked out. I said she just sent a nonsense video and also did not tell my girlfriend . . . but Sam continues to pursue one-on-one hangouts and I'm unsure of how to handle the situation all around. Help?

—LILY, 26

A. I have a feeling Sam knows exactly what she said in the video. She was giving herself an easy out by pretending not to remember. When you lied and said it was just a drunk video, you sidestepped an important and inevitable conversation. Alas, I would have probably done the same thing in your situation.

When someone has feelings for me that I don't reciprocate, I let it ride for as long as possible and hope they'll read my energy or change their mind. Calling out someone's crush feels unnecessarily harsh to me, especially when most crushes are benign and inconsequential. Your situation is different, though. Sam is not a casual acquaintance or someone you mostly interact with online; she's your close friend and her actions are jeopardizing your friendship.

Whenever I feel anxious about disappointing or hurting someone, I remember all the times I've been turned down in life and love. It sucks to be rejected, but I survived. The world didn't end. I didn't hate the other person. Remind Sam that you processed your relationship years ago and decided, together, to stay friends. Tell her that you're committed to your friendship with her, as well as to your relationship with your girlfriend. I know how difficult it can be to confront someone you care about, but one awkward conversation is better than avoiding Sam for the rest of your life and letting one drunk video ruin years of friendship. ♥

So, I'm twenty-three and I've never kissed anyone. Or even held hands romantically. I've only recently come to terms with liking women, and I'm not out at all except on the handful of dating apps I downloaded this summer and have since deleted. I did end up going on a date (the first one I've ever been on, at twenty-three!), but we just sat and talked and I ended up ghosting her. I've been diagnosed with social anxiety, and it has gotten better recently thanks to medication, but I can't afford therapy and I don't have anyone that I talk to about . . . well, anything. I'm also not at all conventionally attractive, and I'm pretty fat (which I have no problem with, but I'm acutely aware that other people do), so I've never been approached by anyone, no matter their gender. I guess what I want advice about is, should I try to find a romantic partner now so I can "catch up" with my peers? Because being a virgin who's never kissed anyone, not even as a kid or on a dare or anything, really messes with my sense of self. Like, I'll feel fine and normal, and then suddenly I'm hyperaware that I'm really not. I don't drink or smoke either, so I feel like I really just don't fit in with my peers. I know there are a lot of other people with similar experiences and a lot of "late bloomers," but those people aren't the mainstream, y'know? I'm worried that if I keep getting older but remain inexperienced, then eventually it will be too late. Honestly, all of this is so embarrassing. Should I try to find a girlfriend, even if I'm not super into them? Would you date someone in their twenties who's never even kissed someone? Am I being completely irrational and none of this matters at all? And if so, why do I feel like I would rather die than say the words "I'm a virgin" out loud? I've never talked to anyone about this, so any insight would be really appreciated.

—MAUREEN, 23

A. Late bloomers aren't mainstream, true, but that's because late bloomer culture *is* queer culture. Everyone I know feels like their life is behind schedule, whether it's finishing their degree, getting published, adopting a dog, finding a partner, quitting their day job, etc., etc., on and on forever. Still, I understand why you're feeling down. The word *virgin* holds so much power in our world. There are entire movies premised on the idea that virginity is an embarrassing, shameful state of being that must be shed at all costs. When, really, having sex doesn't change who you are as a person. It does not damage or alter your body forever, nor does it unlock a magical font of wisdom or adulthood. Sex is a life experience like any other. It can be amazing, revelatory, traumatic, weird, boring, or any number of adjectives, but it does not dictate your worth as a human.

If you don't believe me, think about how many different definitions there are of sex. Some people think sex is when a penis penetrates a vagina, and that's it. Anything beyond that, like oral sex or finger banging, doesn't count as "real sex." I asked some queer friends, and they defined sex as having an orgasm with someone else present, or someone else causing you to orgasm. Then they expanded orgasm to feeling pleasure or expressing yourself and your desires through sex. And then someone brought up BDSM and kink, and it all got so complicated. Sex is whatever you want it to be, as long as there's consent between everyone involved. I'm not sure what my personal definition of sex is, but I know when it happens for me. I also think masturbation is a form of sex, as well as a way to explore your sexuality and clarify what you want from partnered experiences.

To be honest, Maureen, the questions you're asking—How do I meet someone? Is it better to be alone than in a relationship with someone I don't really like? How do I manifest the sexual experiences that I want?—are questions almost everyone grapples with throughout their lives. I live in a small city without many queer dating options. On top of that, I don't develop crushes very often. So when I go through a breakup, I'm often plunged into a bleak scarcity mindset where the idea of meeting someone new seems impossible. I've dated so many people because I was lonely, bored, or looking for a distraction. I always end up regretting it. It's a shitty thing to do to someone, and it might prevent you from meeting someone you're actually into or from doing important work on yourself.

You're right about one thing— it can feel impossible to date when you're sober. It's kind of an open secret, but bars and clubs are actually terrible places to meet new people. This is especially true if you're someone who doesn't like unstructured social situations and open-ended conversations. Luckily, if you live in a midsize to large city, chances are there are game nights, sports leagues, crafting groups, and covens that are specifically for queer people. Also, check if there's an LGBTQIA+ center in your area that offers accessible therapy, support groups, or other opportunities to be around other queers. A lot of indie bookstores have queer or feminist book clubs—I joined one when I lived in Portland and it was so chaotic, but I met my friend J who introduced me to his friends, and then we planned a queer arts festival together. There are so many options!! Maybe what I'm saying sounds dorky, but nobody is born with a popping social life. It takes work and effort to bring people into your life, and structured activities remove a lot of the obstacles. When you're held in close proximity by a shared task, you're forced to communicate and find common ground. These activities also occur at a set time, which reduces the chances of people flaking at the last minute.

You also mentioned that you're fat. Fat queers date and fuck and fall in love and build beautiful, dreamy relationships all the time. While fatphobia is as prevalent in queer communities as it is anywhere else, there are queer scenes and tons of amazing babes that are committed to body diversity. So while I want to honor the reality of fatphobia and the complexity of your experiences, please don't let it discourage or intimidate you from putting yourself out into the world.

And, finally, sex seems scary in the abstract. But when it happens with someone who respects and cares about you, you won't need to study beforehand or perfect a technique. You can ask your partner what they want and figure it out as you go along. You can move as slowly as you want and stop at any time. Sex can be weird and funny and surprising. It can help you feel closer to your partner and yourself. But, like a relationship, sex is not something you need in order to be complete. ♥

I'm a baby dyke (just came out) and I think I'm in love with one of my close friends. She's bi and has been kinda flirting with me, but she does this with a lot of my friends (including straight girls) and, like every useless lesbian on the internet, I'm not sure if she actually likes me. Here's where it gets complicated: One of our mutual friends is also in love with her, and they've been best friends for as long as I can remember. He's trans but isn't out to anyone outside our friend group, for safety reasons. He confessed this to me a couple weeks ago and has since been updating me on his efforts to flirt with her, etc. I really like her and I want to ask her on a date, but (1) I'm not sure if she likes me back, (2) I don't want to ruin our friendship, and (3) I feel like I'm betraying my other friend. Please help!!

—ALEXIS, 15

A. Oh to be a baby dyke again! Shaved head, duct tape. Boots for days. And the innocence of being without realizing it yet. We hold a lot of weight as we grow. And it changes the way we feel things. The way we see things. The clarity is superb. And I feel grateful that I can share my support as someone who has transitioned through, and into, Full Dyke Mode.

Your message fills me with the wonder of firsts. Love and crush. And pain and fear. The kind of things that keep us from us. I feel like there are two paths in life, and I see them both developing in your language. One is to continue to imagine others' feelings without knowing how they actually feel, or to write the story of someone else's path without having any evidence of the truth. And the other journey is to stay focused on ONLY where YOU are and what YOU

do. To stay on YOUR path, and to be authentically YOU and honest with your intentions.

Let me translate your message into the language of a forty-one-year-old lesbian who has had a whole lot of therapy:

I'm a young dyke who just came out, and I have feelings for one of my friends. Another one of our friends also likes her and has been talking to me about it. I'm not sure what to do.

See what I did here?

When it comes down to it, life is a lot simpler than we sometimes make it. All you have to do is act with integrity, authenticity, and belief in yourself. You like her. You don't want to fuck up your friendship with either of them, and you will NEVER—I repeat—YOU WILL NEVER KNOW EXACTLY

HOW SOMEONE ELSE FEELS ABOUT YOU!!!! Not even when someone tells you. Fucked up, right? Scary, right? Yeah, believe me, it sucks. There can be a lot of fear around that concept, but there is a whole lot of beauty as well. Because it gives you the opportunity to build up your own self-confidence so that: (1) You always have your self-love, even when you are hurting. (2) You don't try to force someone else to have feelings when they don't. (3) You don't want to be with someone who doesn't want to be with you!!! These are things that took me a very long time to realize and . . . Goddess, I wish someone had just told me straight up.

So, with all of that being said: I would first tell said trans friend (labeling for the sake of clarification), "Hey, friend, I have feelings for ____ too, and I wanted to tell you first because you have been sharing your feelings with me about her, and it felt strange to keep it from you. How do you feel about me saying that?" Or something like that . . .

What happens next is a beautiful mystery of life. There are soooooo many possible responses. Dude may say, "OMG that's awesome. Go for it." Or Dude may say, "HAHA well, I guess we can just see what happens." Or Dude might say, "SHIT, that sucks . . . I'm really upset." Or he may say, "Cool, let's see if she is interested in a throuple!" Your job after talking to him is to ONLY control your OWN behavior. So think about all the possible options and how they make you feel and how you would best want to respond. Maybe even write it all down if you want to get super clear with yourself and your intentions.

If he is upset, then it may be good to hold off on moving forward, and emphasize your desire to keep things good with y'all. He will probably feel more confident in your relationship and trust you even more in the future. If he tells her what you said, who cares . . . it is your truth, after all. Or, you could say, "I really like her, and I know it may ruin our friendship, but I think I still want to ask her out."

And he can feel whatever the fuck he wants and act however he wants to act. You can't control him. You can only control you. It might be hard not to react, but you knew it might be difficult, so you have to just allow him to feel his feelings and you to feel yours. If your relationship with him is super important to you, then I say, move on, young one. There are more dykes in the pit.

Now, we begin to see some clarity in ourselves once we let go of the concept that we can just have whatever we want whenever we want it. Specifically, that this woman should need to choose between you two. She may not be interested in either of you, or anyone at all right now; maybe her flirtation is really just her personality. Allow that to just be her. Not a request for attention. Or a desire to fuck. She is merely fun and enjoys people and is optimistic and loves connection. And if she is flirting, maybe that is just what she does. If you judge that now, take a hard look at the way you might treat her as a partner.

Next up, if you like her and your friend tells you that it's cool to go for it, then be honest with her that you have feelings for her, AND that your friendship means a lot to you. If she isn't interested, you can try to stay on track with your relationship as is. With all the new self-love and awareness you are

drumming up, there's no way you would want anything with someone who doesn't want it with you. It may be awkward for a little bit, but just stay being your rad self and I'm sure in time everything will be A-OK. If she is interested in moving forward with you . . . just stick to the rest of my advice about being a good person. Learn to love yourself first. Stay on your side of the street, and be the best human you can be. What other people think (or say) about you is actually none of your business.

As a baby dyke, every single second seems like forever, but there is something really powerful in being patient and taking some time just for you.

Think about what you really want for your life in this moment. If it is sex and fun, then I bet you can find it from someone outside of your friend group. It would be awesome to have support and love and friendship around you when things get complicated in your heart. ❤

—JD SAMSON
Musician & Guest Expert

P.S. I say this with the most love that I possibly can: Please never call yourself (or any other lesbian) "useless." We all have our purpose, and the right to be exactly who we are.

THE WEBS
WE WEAVE

RELATIONSHIPS & DATING

CHAPTER TWO

As a queer advice writer, I'm often asked: What kinds of questions and concerns do people send in to *The Ex-Girlfriend of My Ex-Girlfriend Is My Girlfriend*? Without hard analysis, I would say the most common questions boil down to "My open relationship is stressing me out," "My long-distance relationship is stressing me out," and "I've never had sex" or "I've had less sex than I think is normal for someone my age." Close runners-up are "coming out later in life," "my girlfriend is close friends with her ex and it makes me feel insecure," and "I went through a breakup ages ago and I can't seem to meet anyone new." Lots of people are withholding secrets from their partner, struggling to find queer community, or in love with a close friend. I receive tons of questions from monogamous people considering open relationships, but I have yet to receive a question from a non-monogamous person considering a closed relationship.

When I respond to questions, I often feel like Gay Debbie Downer. I'm tempering someone's expectations for life and love—nobody is born with an amazing group of friends, it takes a lot of work to be comfortable with yourself, and it's normal to be sad for a long time after a breakup. Your deep, dark source of shame and embarrassment is probably pretty normal. As Solange tells us in "Cranes in the Sky," everyone has times in their life when they feel interminably lonely, miserable, and stuck. Also, perhaps because I was single for the making of this book, I noticed that tons of questions depicted being single as a bleak, irredeemable hell. I wish people would open their imaginations to the possibilities of being single. Actually, I wish people would open their imaginations to the possibilities of life in general. This chapter is my attempt to help you do just that.

Q. **So, my girlfriend and I** have been dating long distance for the last year. Luckily, we have been able to see each other quite frequently (around every three weeks) for most of it. She is hands down the most intelligent, open-minded, beautiful person I have ever met, inside and out. The only thing is, she has had many more sexual partners/general sexual experiences than I have. It does not affect our (amazing) sexual relationship, but it does make me feel a bit insecure about myself sometimes. She is very open about sex and will casually announce when we are/she is in the presence of someone who she has slept with. I am a bit of a demisexual and have only slept with people I have dated and have absolutely no contact with now. I sometimes find myself wishing that I had done the same thing she did before we were dating, or feeling like maybe I am missing out on something. It's kind of like a ridiculous FOMO feeling; I'm not sure if I genuinely feel that way or if it's just my insecurity getting the best of me when it is brought up. We both have discussed how we don't want an open relationship. Sooooo, any ideas on how to get over the insecurity of sexual inexperience???

—LUCIA, 22

A. When I think of someone who's sexually experienced, I picture someone who can confidently communicate their boundaries and desires. I imagine someone who respects and listens to their partner. It's a skill set that requires intention and care to cultivate, not unlike gardening or Kansas City–style BBQ. It's not as simple as having a high body count—if you need proof, think about all the cis straight men who live to fuck and have never once made a woman come.

unworthy is a sign that your partner is undermining your self-esteem or purposefully creating an unbalanced power dynamic. This might be something to reflect on or discuss with your girlfriend.

With sex, as with all things, it can be difficult to distinguish what you actually want from what you think you *should* want. You admire and love your girlfriend. It makes sense that when she waxes poetic about past hookups, you feel like your life is lacking in comparison. But you and your girlfriend are different people with different approaches to sex and relationships. At the same time, I wonder: Do you ever feel like your girlfriend is trying to make you feel insecure? Sometimes, feeling inadequate and

To be honest, Lucia, it sounds like you know yourself really well. You're someone who prefers to have sex in the context of a monogamous relationship. That may not always be the case—in the future, your FOMO might call you to date three women at once, fall in love with a beautiful stranger, or go where the wind takes you. But for right now, you have a clear sense of what makes you uncomfortable when it comes to relationships and sex. You don't need to change who you are for your girlfriend, or for anyone. ♥

Q. **The girl I've been dating** for the last five months has a near-perfect body, and it has launched me into negative and unhealthy thinking about my own body. She has a six-pack without really trying, she eats without too much care (she loves butter and candy), and is just generally really comfortable in her skin. She is extremely vocally affirmative about being attracted to me, so that isn't the issue; it's just that, sometimes, I look at her body and feel mine wanting to shrink. I feel like a big amorphous blob. She is basically this gallant, lean horse gleaming in the sun, and I feel like her dusty, overfed donkey companion. It makes me less present in sex, and I know how unat-tractive self-consciousness can be. I don't want my own body issues to impact our dynamic, and I especially don't want to blame her; I know it's me who is constantly making the comparison. How can I get back to loving my body—a place I've worked hard to get to in the past? Is this just an early relationship acclimation that I'll be able to get past?

—KARMA, 29

A. I know a lot of women like your girlfriend—women with blissful, uncomplicated relationships to food and their bodies. I live in awe of them. I cannot imagine what it would be like to just exist in my body.

For most of my teens and early twenties, my weight was the first thing I thought about when I woke up and the last thing on my mind when I fell asleep at night. I wouldn't allow myself to go to the beach, get a haircut, or buy new clothes unless I was at or below my ideal weight. Everyone in my life encouraged this. I've since gone to therapy and done tons of painful, difficult work on myself, but there will always be a part of me that only feels safe when I hate my body. It's like I'm this confident, independent woman who acquired a pack of gremlins in the fifth grade and sometimes I go to use the bathroom and they're just sitting on the toilet, and I'm like, *Oh my god, HOW DID YOU GET IN HERE?* And all at once the gremlins turn to look at me and say, "WE NEVER LEFT."

I'm so grateful you sent me this question, Karma—not because you're struggling, but because it's SO ISOLATING to be a queer woman with body image issues. When I try to talk to my friends and partners about my struggles, I'm almost always dismissed with clichés like "You should love yourself!" and "Your body is a miracle." It feels like I'm bumming everyone out. Also, since so many people struggle with disordered eating and body image, it's not a topic I can bring up in casual conversation. I understand and respect this, but it can contribute to a sense of shame or embarrassment.

Right now, you're conceptualizing your body image issues and insecurities as personal failures. What would happen if you thought of them as mechanisms that keep you safe? For me, body-hatred is a fallback when something good happens for me. It's a way for me to self-sabotage and impose limits on myself. New relationships bring up bad body feelings for me, but so do important life achievements and celebrations when I know others will be looking at me and taking my picture. My brain can counteract anything

positive and joyful with a sneak attack of weight obsession. Ask yourself: What kind of situations and feelings make me feel self-conscious about my body or like I can't stop comparing myself to my girlfriend?

Maybe none of this is relevant for you. Body image is so complicated, and healing is different for everyone. I wish I had more concrete, solid tips for you. I wish I had more concrete, solid tips for myself. I know you're already getting affirmations of hotness from your girlfriend, but I also want to add that you are a hot, powerful horse with a perfect body. When you feel like a donkey, it's just gremlins trying to sabotage your happiness. ♥

I'm a gay girl at a small liberal arts school in Ohio. Almost a year ago I became involved with a friend of mine, but things eventually ended when she went abroad. We kept in touch (sometimes daily, sometimes sexually) while she was gone, but there was no explicit expectation that anything would resume when she returned, although it often felt that way. When this school year started, it became clear through friends that she had a long-distance boyfriend from abroad. I was really disappointed, and felt equally frustrated with her and myself for the lapse in communication. I started seeing a new girl and things got serious really quickly. This time all my needs are completely met, especially in terms of sex and communication. She makes me really happy, and I care about her. And of course, I feel like a complete clown because I can't stop thinking about the girl who went abroad, who has given me close to nothing for nearly a year, was generally shady, etc. Her relationship with her boyfriend is starting to deteriorate, and she's started reaching out more again. I know she'll never tell me explicitly how she feels. Is it worth sacrificing my new situation for a bunch of hypothetical, open-ended drama? Am I being a terrible person? An idiot? I just want to deal with this in the least messy way possible.

—JANE, 20

A. I hate to be the one who tells you this, Jane, but people who send mixed signals are hot. People who text us one day and ignore us the next, whose words and actions we must decipher and decode, are REALLY, REALLY HOT. They are so hot, they should be reprimanded. "But why, Maddy?" you might ask. "Why are they hot? Why am I so into my flighty ex?" There are many possible reasons. Perhaps you feel undeserving of a caring, healthy relationship. Maybe you've been conditioned by mainstream culture to view queer relationships as inherently dysfunctional. Or maybe you learned as a child that love is something you must constantly earn and work for, and now you're an adult who becomes suspicious and scared when a relationship feels too easy. It could simply be that you're not invested in your current relationship and your ex is offering an easy out. The reasons why we choose the relationships and partners that we do are complicated, and building healthy, honest relationships is a lifetime's work.

I have a feeling you're spending a lot of time stalking your ex's social media. You're also receiving a lot of gossip from your friends. No wonder you can't move on. Trying to discern and puzzle together someone's intentions and feelings is a full-time job. It's exhausting and consuming in a way that direct, honest communication is not.

The first thing you need to do is decide what kind of relationship you want with your ex. Then

you need to talk to her, face to face if possible, and establish some boundaries. You didn't process anything before she went abroad, so now you're faced with a doubly difficult task: understanding what you had before and deciding what you want moving forward. If you decide to pursue a romantic relationship, she needs to make major amendments to her behavior. You need to be prepared to hold her account-able. If you decide to be friends or neutral acquaintances, however, clearing the air will remove a lot of the anxiety and unknown when you inevitably cross paths on campus.

You're in charge of your own life. I hope you don't tank your current relationship for someone who's been nothing but careless with your feelings and time. As Maya Angelou once said, "When someone shows you who they are, believe them the first time." 💜

I am newly in a long-distance open relationship with someone I used to see practically every day. It's been tough, as it's my first long-term, long-distance, and open relationship. We're on the same page about open relationship stuff, but nothing has happened yet. We got into our first phone fight about unrelated friend drama. But basically I'm worried about communication. I feel that I am a good communicator, but I have a harder time sorting through my feelings and knowing what my boundaries are than my girlfriend does. When I'm upset I interpret things she says differently than the way she means them and work myself up into getting more upset. I'm worried that might get difficult in an open relationship when things do happen with other people. I want advice on communicating in long-distance relationships and practical communication skills that might help, if you happen to know any.

—L, 23

A. Your relationship is transitioning from same-city to long-distance, and from monogamous to open, all at the same time. Honestly, I'd be surprised if you and your girlfriend weren't experiencing some strain.

When you misinterpret your girlfriend's words, are you using conflict as a defense mechanism? Are you instigating fights because you're worried she might hurt you? The first time "things happen" in an open relationship can bring on some intense feelings of jealousy, abandonment, and rejection. It's normal to feel apprehensive or scared. A lot of people discover over the course of their first open relationship that they're okay with nonmonogamy in theory, but not in practice.

But you asked specifically about communication in long-distance relationships. I have been in several LDRs and my number-one tip is to shore up your communication. Instead of texting constantly throughout the day, schedule FaceTime or phone sessions. This doesn't have to be a strict, immovable appointment. If something exciting happens and you want to text your girlfriend, you should! But by being a little more intentional about your communication, you can ensure that you and your girlfriend stay engaged and present in your daily lives. It will also give you

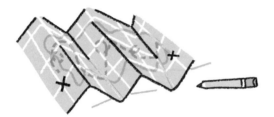

the space and time to foster new relationships, and ensure that the onus of texting first or initiating a phone conversation doesn't fall on just one of you.

When you love someone who lives far away, there's a lot of pressure for your in-person visits to be fun and sexy. Travel is expensive, and no matter how much you want to see each other, scheduling can be a nightmare. When you finally get to be together, the last thing either of you wants is to process or have a difficult conversation about your relationship. As a result, there's a tendency for all your pent-up feelings to explode once you're apart. The best way to prevent this is regular, scheduled check-ins where you talk about the health of your relationship. Also, be mindful not to build a mystique around your girlfriend now that she's far away. She's the same person. You're the same person. You're both just people, doing your best in the face of change. ♥

Q. **I used to be able to spend** so much time alone, but now I have been swept into the tunnel of love and am finding alone time increasingly rare. I enjoy every loving and fighting and fickle fleeting moment with my partner, and I can't seem to tear myself away. How do I regain my sense of self now that somebody else has infiltrated it and I feel the tug in both directions? It's making me insecure. Can you help?

—GRETCHEN, 33

A. The tunnel of love is beautiful, but it can also be unsettling and vulnerable. You're someone who finds a lot of comfort and serenity in being alone. You need space to process and adjust to new emotions. Tell your partner you need some time apart, even if it's just a night or a weekend. Even if part of you likes the constant togetherness, the last thing you want is to lash out at your partner because you're overwhelmed and on the brink of an existential crisis. Time apart will make your relationship more sustainable. ♥

Q. **I have struggled with mental health** problems (depression, anxiety, self-harm, eating disorder, PTSD) since adolescence, and they have recently begun coming back. I first want to state that I do have a therapist who I see semi-regularly and am on medication, so this question isn't asking you to be a mental health professional at all!!! My girlfriend and I have been dating for about two years, and she is aware to some extent of my history and current struggles. I just really don't know how much to share with her and what to share with her. I want to be honest and not leave her in the dark about what I'm dealing with, but I also don't want to overwhelm her, or worry her, or any of that. She doesn't really have mental health issues herself, so I know that she doesn't always know how to respond to the things I tell her. We have pretty good communication, but I also don't want to put her in a place where she feels any type of way (like I don't want to overwhelm her or make her uncomfortable, I guess??). I also think I feel ashamed that I'm still dealing with some of these problems. I just don't know how to skate the line of being open with her, but also not putting her in a position that she wouldn't be able to handle (like not making her my therapist I guess, and keeping her from feeling overwhelmed).

—ELLIOT, 24

A. I imagine there have been times in your life when you felt totally defined by your mental health problems, like all your relationships and interactions were colored by a narrative you had no control over. I also imagine that you've experienced the intense stigma surrounding mental illness firsthand—at the very least, you've had a friend undermine your use of medication or say "PTSD" in a joking manner. There are so many reasons for your fears and apprehension.

What stands out to me about your question is that you and your girlfriend have been together for two years. That's a long time! I would be surprised if your girlfriend hasn't already noticed that you're struggling or acting differently. She might be unsure of how to help or think that she's somehow to blame. Maybe she won't be able to relate exactly to what you're going through, but she won't understand anything unless you let her in.

If you're concerned about using your girlfriend as a therapist,

let her know that you already have a support system in place. Tell her it's not her responsibility to help you. Talk about each other's needs and boundaries. Don't be afraid to ask for support—it's not unlike if your girlfriend had a severe bee allergy and she asked you to carry an EpiPen and learn to recognize the symptoms of anaphylactic shock.

One of the most terrifying things about being human is that the people we love are not obligated to stay with us. We can censor and contort ourselves to be easier and more palatable. We can go to therapy and make deep transformations in our thoughts and actions. But we can never guarantee that the people we love will stick around. I'm not writing this to scare you, just to say that you can't control how your girlfriend reacts. All you can do is your best. Keep going to therapy, taking your meds, and showing yourself the same empathy and care that you show your girlfriend. ♥

I'm new to poly (I'm sure you get that a lot) and have been having a tough time setting boundaries with my primary partner. For context, I'm her primary partner too. We aren't making "rules" as much as discussing personal boundaries and establishing shared values. One of my boundaries is that I'd prefer that my girlfriend not date my best friends (five, specifically) or my sister. I've said that her developing feelings for them also makes me uncomfy, but is less avoidable. Recently, my girlfriend fell in love with my best friend, who is also her roommate. The webs we weave! She decided to tell my friend, even though we knew my friend wasn't interested, and even though I asked her to keep discussing the best approach with me. She went ahead and did it anyway, so obviously I am angry. This is the *second* time almost this exact situation has happened. She claims it's because she's polyanarchical, and she wants her partners to be open to her dating their friends "if the relationship progresses that way." Honestly,

I just want her to deal with her feelings earlier and kinda shut it down instead of blowing up our whole social scene for unrequited love. I also think it's a reasonable boundary for me not to want her to date members of my closest support system, because it feels destabilizing when it inevitably blows up. Are we actually incompatible or should we be compromising somehow?

—YARA, 25

A. This question unmoored me to the point that I had to shut my laptop, get in my car, and take myself to the nearest Taco Bell drive-thru. I'm back now. I'm shaking the chalupa crumbs out of my bra, and I'm ready to write your response.

If I've learned one thing in my life, it's that it's a big red flag when someone uses polyamory, or one of its many variations, as an excuse to do whatever they want. At the end of the day, your partner agreed to one set of boundaries, violated those boundaries, and then refused to take responsibility for her actions.

Are you incompatible? Should you be compromising? All relationships have conflict. All relationships require compromise. But the extent to which you're willing to undergo conflict and compromise is something only you can decide. ♥

My current partner is wonderful, trustworthy, understanding, patient, and communicative, and very clearly loves me a lot. This is my first relationship since a multiyear abusive relationship, and my first queer relationship ever. In general, even though we live an hour apart, things are amazing and my partner is the perfect person to have by my side on my healing journey. Except for one thing: I struggle with debilitating jealousy. My partner is still friends with their exes, and sure I get a small twinge of jealousy when they hang out, but my fixation is on one of their roommates. They are best friends and slept together more than once a few months before we became monogamous. I know intellectually I have nothing to worry about—our relationship is strong, and I believe them when they say they are not interested in pursuing anything with their roommate again—but emotionally I can't help but spiral and obsess. I've been working on it and talking to my therapist about it for a while, but I haven't been able to obsess less. It's affecting my comfort being at their apartment when their roommate is there, my ability to be friendly with their roommate, and my peace of mind when we're apart (not to mention how much my partner worries about it, even after I've told them it's my responsibility to deal with). What can I do to combat my jealousy? Or SHOULD I do anything to combat my jealousy? Am I right to be worried? How can I keep this from being a relationship-ending problem?

GUEST EXPERT • SAMANTHA IRBY

A. I am so very sorry to be the asshole who says this to you, BUT: It sounds like this is a relationship-ending problem! Listen, I understand the desire to be "cool." I spent my entire dating life in my twenties pretending to be "chill" and "confident" and "secure" and "low-key" and all the other trap descriptors we're taught to aspire to in order to get sex and trick someone into texting us back until we finally feel safe enough (i.e., are reasonably sure they are tangled enough in our web to not bolt immediately) to be our real selves around them. And, if your real self is jealous and insecure, maybe you shouldn't be in a relationship with a person who lives with someone they used to have sex with. You're not chill! And that is absolutely okay! But you also shouldn't force yourself to stay in a relationship that brings out the worst in you.

In a perfect world, everyone could afford their own fucking apartment, and you wouldn't be sitting at home worrying yourself sick thinking about your partner brushing their teeth in their underwear with their smoldering sexpot of a roommate hovering breathlessly outside the bathroom door. In a perfect world, you wouldn't be an hour away grinding your molars to stumps at the thought that they might share a lusty, lingering glance, their fingertips accidentally brushing against each other in the lukewarm water, while washing soapy wine glasses at the sink. In a perfect world you could eat a bucket of popcorn while watching your partner engage in *actual* sexual intercourse with another person without the slightest twinge of jealousy because you are so confident both in your feelings for them and in their absolute loyalty to you—but here's the thing: This world? It's far from perfect! And you are a jealous person who cannot handle their partner's ex-sex friends.

What are you telling your therapist? What is the therapist saying back to you? Isn't one of the objects of therapy to give you tools to use during the many hours of the week in which you are not in the therapist's office? Are you lying to the therapist? Are you not listening to the sound and educated and practical advice (I assume) the therapist is giving you? How long is "a while?" How long is too long to be seeing a therapist who doesn't seem to actually be helping you solve your problems? Seriously, though, are you telling the therapist the whole truth? Do you listen when the therapist tells you something you don't want to hear, or do you leave their office and just do whatever you were gonna

do in the first place? How did you find this therapist? Why haven't they helped you? Isn't it weird that you are having an ongoing conversation with a professional about an emotional response you are having to a person you honestly don't need to be romantically entangled with? Why are you wasting your copay on a therapist if you're willing to accept advice from me, a comedy writer who barely graduated high school????

Jealousy is a natural emotion (except in the extreme!), and unless yours is manifesting itself in an unhealthy way (you aren't secretly following them around in your car or printing out reams of sent text messages to decipher them for clues, are you?), I don't know that you really have to do anything to combat it. I mean, what even could you do? It's so clear, to me at least, that if you understand intellectually that a person you say you believe and have described as "trustworthy," "communicative," and "wonderful" has no desire to cheat, then maybe you just shouldn't be in a relationship with that person because the

problem here is yours. If your partner is a person who is going to remain friends with some exes and live in the bedroom next door to others, and that's a thing you can't handle, then why force yourself to handle it? It's hard for me to say what I really want to say because the words "healing journey" make me feel like I should tread lightly, but if you are spiraling over a situation you can't control that concerns two people an hour away who insist upon living together despite the fact that it preys on your insecurities and sends you into a fucking tailspin and you can't stop obsessing about it in therapy and boring your friends with it and compromising your peace of mind because of it, nagging your partner with it and snarling at their roommate every time they're in close proximity because wow your jealousy is just so out of control, ummm, why do you need to do that??? YOU DON'T. ❤

—SAMANTHA IRBY
Writer & Guest Expert

THE UNIVERSE NEEDS TO APOLOGIZE

HEARTBREAK

CHAPTER THREE

A long time ago, I had a minor fling that ended in a string of terse, vaguely hostile text messages. Logically, I knew that this woman and I did not have a lot in common. We did not share the same sense of humor or live in the same time zone. Our relationship was not meant to go the distance. But I still thought about her all the time. Two years passed, and I was still stalking her Instagram on the daily. I craved her attention and approval. I was experiencing a level of distress and turmoil that was totally disproportionate to the reality of our relationship. Compared to other heartbreaks and romantic disappointments, I didn't do much in the way of intentionally moving on, either. I didn't buy a loom or shave my head or sign up for capoeira classes. I didn't go on a million first dates, though, to be fair, I live in a small city and finding other queer women to date is a struggle. Eventually, something inside me just let go.

When I'm giving advice about heartbreak or breakups, I often prescribe strict boundaries and refocused energy. But, ultimately, it just takes time to get your breath back. The questions in this chapter are all about the darker side of love.

Q. **A girl broke my heart** after nearly two years of song-and-dance flirting; whatever, it happens. The problem is we run in the same, relatively small professional circles and, dammit, we're grown-ups. What is a grown-up sup-posed to do here? I haven't told any of our mutual friends, because that seems like unnecessary drama, but also I am not interested in spending time with others around her. She hurt me, and I don't want to keep pretending it's fine. This friend/professional group lives across the US, so it's not like it's a daily problem. Do I just have to suck it up and accept that, as experience repeatedly proves, every academic conference will involve awkward encounters with exes?

—BERU, 30

A. I once had a painful, unrequited crush on a woman I met on Instagram. Although it was possible for us to hang out in real life, we exclusively texted and talked over FaceTime. I thought about her constantly. I even told her I liked her. Her response was oblique and slippery. Her general texting style was hot and cold. Still, I kept trying to get her attention. This went on for a year. Ultimately, I instigated a weird fight over text and immediately apologized because I felt embarrassed. Looking back, I regret not saying something like, "I wish you had been honest and transparent about your feelings. I feel manipulated and hurt." It would have given me a sense of finality and permission to grieve.

It's so, so hard to find closure from someone you never actually dated. Everyone understands the word *breakup*. But it can be difficult to describe a prolonged flirtation defined by mixed signals and disappointment. If this girl were someone you saw on a regular basis, you'd have an immunity toward her.

But since you only see her at conferences, she becomes this huge, looming presence on the horizon. All you can do is remind yourself that she's just a person. She doesn't deserve your anxiety or concern. Luckily, time is a powerful balm. Seeing her will get easier and easier with each passing conference. ♥

Q. **My recent ex-girlfriend,** having no connection to my ex-girlfriend of many years ago—they've never met, and my prior ex caused me tremendous pain—decided to become her Instagram friend days after we broke up, and now they comment on each other's posts all the time. I know my only reasonable choice is to ignore it and move on, but I had hoped we'd become friends someday, and this move on her part makes me question her judgment now and wonder if I can ever trust her in the future. Is there anything I can do to protect myself from their drama?

—LEE, 45

A. This is a rare situation where the only reasonable course of action is also the best revenge. I'm talking, of course, about emotionally disengaging and not looking at content that makes you feel like garbage. You must stop checking your ex-girlfriends' Instagrams imme-diately. Some methods include: Make a tally on a sheet of paper for every twelve hours you go without Instastalking them, download an app that blocks the internet, or leave the house without your phone. Hide their profiles from your feed. Delete them from your search history. Sleep with your phone across the room, so you're not sucked in first thing in the morning. Delete Instagram from your phone if you must.

You must be intentional, brave, and steadfast. Some days will be harder than others, but soon you will unlearn the muscle memory and compulsion to look at your ex-girlfriends' posts. As a bumper sticker I once read said: *Let go and let goddess.* ♥

Q. Recently my girlfriend of a year and a half broke up with me. Things had been ehh for a little bit, and we ultimately broke up because I felt like she didn't want to be in the relationship anymore. I spent a lot of time reflecting and processing (yay therapy), but I still have unresolved feelings. I know she doesn't hate me and that our relationship did in fact mean something to her, but I am still unsure of why we broke up. I have asked my ex what changed, but every time I ask she says she doesn't know and that it wasn't me, she just felt different. The problem is that I don't understand how that happened. When we broke up I was still very much in love with her, and I don't understand how her feelings could have changed without it being my fault or without me doing something to make them change. How do I stop obsessing over this and move on?

—VANESSA, 21

A. Sometimes relationships end for a concrete, singular reason—your girlfriend lies to you, moves across the country, or hurts you in a big way. But most of the time, relationships end for a series of complex reasons that are difficult to comprehend, let alone put into words. In my experience, the former makes it easier to establish distance and move on—at least at first.

It's normal to want an explanation when a relationship ends. But the truth is that sometimes feelings just change, especially when you're twenty-one and still discovering important parts of yourself. Sometimes you grow apart from someone, or you realize that the two of you have completely different expectations and needs from a relationship.

Right now, you're giving your ex undue power over your life and feelings. You cannot depend on her for permission to move on. Instead, you have to alchemize your own closure out of thin air. The first step is to find some distance. If you're still communicating and spending time together, try one month without any contact. Stay far, far away from her social media. Don't feel guilty about blocking her if it helps you move on. When you feel the urge to text her, text a friend instead. Or better yet, message someone you're interested in knowing better. Throw a dinner party. Take a weekend trip. Dye your hair. Buy fifty-seven houseplants. All of this will feel like checking off boxes, or like you're going through the motions. This is because you're doing work, Vanessa—the work of preparing for a new relationship, a relationship with someone who unequivocally, enthusiastically loves being with you and doesn't make you feel insecure.

You will have good days and days where everything feels pointless, because the only thing you want is to get your old relationship back. But over time, it will get easier. I promise. ♥

How do you stop self-sabotaging? I've been (mostly) out and dating women for the last few years, and am starting to notice a pattern in myself. Sometimes I get into these weird, shitty moods, and I can feel it affecting whoever I'm dating because I get really quiet and have a hard time expressing myself. My mood can turn from happy to unhappy seemingly without warning. What's worse, I feel it happening but I can't stop myself. Rationally, I know that there's no reason for me to be upset—it could be over a small change in plans, my partner feeling tired and not wanting to sleep over, etc. Little, inconsequential things. I'm currently in a relationship that makes me really happy, after being in some tumultuous ones in the past. My partner makes me feel seen and cared for, the sex is amazing, and I've been having a great time exploring our many similar interests. The last few months have been wonderful, but now my weird mood swings are starting to come back. Am I purposely trying to ruin a good thing?

—CATHRYN, 25

A. When I first read your question, I thought maybe you were describing what it feels like to fall out of love. It can be unnerving when our feelings for someone begin to diminish and fade, especially when there's not a specific reason or cause that we can point to.

What matters, though, is that you are identifying your mood swings as self-sabotage. There's a part of you that wants to create distance between yourself and your girlfriend. So many things could be up! Maybe you don't feel like you deserve a fulfilling relationship with great sex. Maybe commitment and feeling accountable to another human is scary for you. Or you're someone who has very high expectations for your partners, and you begin to resent them when they don't live up to your expectations. All of these things could be connected to self-sabotage, or it could simply be that you're not ready for a relationship right now.

Sometimes when I feel inordinately prickly or annoyed by someone I'm dating, it's because I feel vulnerable or emotionally overextended. Other times, it's just a sign that I need some alone time. It's a stereotype, but queer women do tend to go all in when it comes to relationships and quality time. I am no exception. I have to be careful because even when I enjoy being around someone, it can be exhausting to spend big blocks of unmitigated time with them. I often think about how if I ever

got married, I would want to live in separate apartments in the same building. Maybe we could live on a farm and I could put an RV inside the barn. At the very least, I would want to maintain separate bedrooms.

All this is to say that if you find yourself sliding into a bad mood, ask yourself if you're actually feeling any other emotions, like insecurity, vulnerability, or fear. Do some research into attachment theory. Instead of judging yourself, remember that most people self-sabotage to protect themselves from getting hurt. ♥

I moved to a small and conservative city I had never been to and knew nothing about for a dreamy job. The culture shock fucked me up, and I used romantic connection as a way to find meaning, hope, and kindness in a world I felt suffocated by. After two years passed and two serious relationships ended, I managed to fall in love again. This person and I built a love that felt cosmic to me, like we were brought together to heal ourselves alongside the other. I felt we were made of the same material, just in different vessels. The relationship ended suddenly—unexpectedly from my perspective—after only three months, initiated by them. All polite ways of dancing around the fact that I got dumped. It's been a year, and I am still feeling so mangled. I've been single the whole time and haven't felt any resonance with anyone since, despite bringing a lot of openness and sincerity to meeting other people and trying to expand my world here. With each previous breakup I've had, I was always saddened and

disappointed, but I had faith that there was more love out there in the world, for me—for everyone. I always felt steady in my ability to integrate pain. This time, it's different. How can I accept being alone?

—GENEVA, 32

A. You have a dreamy job—and I'm sure you've had some not-so-dreamy jobs in the past, Geneva, so I don't have to tell you that it's a rare, rare privilege to find work that both sustains you financially and fulfils you emotionally. But you're a whole-ass person, and work is just one aspect of your life. Just like living in a city with a viable queer dating pool might not solve all your problems but can be a source of satisfaction and joy. Something I've noticed about my own life that may or may not be applicable to yours: When my work life is abounding with opportunities, my love life is a real *Silent Spring*. And when my love life is simmering, my work life is a mess. It's almost like the universe apologizes for one deficit by making up for it somewhere else.

But back to your question: how to be alone. I live in Boring, Wisconsin. There are not many queer people where I live, let alone available queer women. Long ago, I accepted that my dating life would be long-distance and facilitated by the internet. This is not ideal for many reasons, namely that plane tickets are expensive and long-distance relationships are often a mirage of mutual projections and fantasies. But once I accepted my lot in lesbian dating hell, I could focus my energy on dating apps and DM-sliding and visiting friends in big cities.

At the time that I'm writing this, I've been single for about a year. Like you, I'm grappling with the fear that I'll never fall in love again. There are moments when I'm so stuck in the weeds that I seriously consider packing up my dog and houseplants and moving to gayer pastures. But when I zoom out and look at my life in the long term, I realize that I could fill an entire city with the lovers and friends that came into my life with zero warning— people so amazing, I never could have imagined them for myself. Have you ever experienced a feeling of wonder and astonishment at the very beginning of a relationship because, just days before, you didn't even know this person? That's because life is unpredictable, and as clichéd as it sounds, none of us know what's going to happen next. ♥

 **Myself and my ex** (we'll call her J) met online as teenagers. She sent me a message that just said "wow ur cute," and that was the beginning of our friendship. It was wonderful; there was never anything romantic at the start, but we quickly became best friends. We lived on different sides of the world, so we Skyped almost daily (I still remember the first call we ever had). And texted pretty much constantly. After becoming friends I couldn't imagine my life without her. We'd always finish each other's sentences and scream "PLATONIC SOULMATES" at each other before descending into fits of giggles. We weren't entirely wrong—the first two to three years were purely platonic, and we were just genuinely best friends. Then we started joking about moving in together and getting married. Just jokes. Maybe. Things started getting a bit more complicated from then on. After about a year of denial, I finally admitted to myself that I had very strong feelings for her, but I refused to say anything for fear of ruining what we had. So I locked it away and continued being her best friend. Around that

time though, things started getting more and more blurry between us. Our friendly ILY!!!s turned into late-night I-love-yous, we started talking seriously about the future, if we could have one, and I suddenly realized, *Holy shit I'm in love with this girl.*

We hit a rough patch after that. When she graduated from high school, she sorta disappeared; she deleted her social media and eventually she stopped even talking to me. I'd been traumatized once before by a childhood best friend ghosting me out of nowhere, so this really put me in a bad place—but I decided to slap on a brave face and get on with my life.

In private though, it was a different story . . . I spent countless nights drunk and alone, crying about a girl I thought would be in my life forever, even platonically—I didn't care, I just needed her by my side. I felt lost without her. I missed everything about her: her laugh, her stupid jokes, the way she said my name, our dumb inside jokes. It was heartbreak.

Eventually I stopped crying (or at least I didn't cry as much), and I let her go. I told myself if it's meant to be, the Universe will bring us back together. I had no choice but to believe that.

About eight months later, I get a message on Tumblr from a blog I don't recognize.

The message starts "holy shit hi, it's me," and I knew exactly who it was. I read through the message about fifteen times, making sure this just wasn't yet another dream I was having about her. It was very real, and slowly we started talking again. It wasn't like it was before, at least not straight away, but I had my girl back and I couldn't have been happier.

Fast-forward to last April, 4/20 to be exact, and I'm sitting on a balcony watching the sunset in Tenerife, feeling pretty great about life. I'm texting J, and all of a sudden we're confessing our feelings to each other. It's such a rush of emotion, and I'm so happy. I won't give any boring details of our relationship; I was head over heels in love, I thought the feeling was mutual.

Long story short, we broke up after five months because J says she doesn't even feel like it's a relationship. And I'll be honest, the final couple months felt very one-sided, at least from my own perspective—I can't speak for J or how she felt toward the end.

It's been over a year now since we've broken up, and I'm still stuck on her. It feels like how it felt the first time, only worse. I'm quite a spiritual person, and I fully believe we're Soulmates, if not Twin Flames. I know she's supposed to be in my life, and if I'm right, then she'll return when we're both ready. And if I'm not right, well hopefully I'll be in a better place by then.

Am I foolish for feeling this way? I've always been pretty good at getting over my exes; I usually keep a wall up and can predict when the end is coming. Whatever it is about J, my heart refuses to let go of her.

—MOONIE, 22

GUEST EXPERT • LOLA PELLEGRINO

A. Dear Moonie,
Are you sure you and I aren't Twin Flames? I write from Lanzarote, an island close to Tenerife, the place you watched the sun set not knowing that in like twenty minutes it would also be setting on your relationship with J, plunging you back into the babeless night.

I'm here with my Forever Girl-friend, also an internet advice columnist who likes to work on vacation, so I started to share your query out loud. Halfway through, Lucinda stopped me.

"Wait, have they met?"

I don't know and *I don't care.*
God, is my girlfriend *even gay?*

Let's say you've never touched J's face. Let's even say you're being Catfished. Moonie, you and I are not straight. Thus we are part of an Alternative Lifestyle, excluded from the world-dominating cishet-only romance narrative, leaving us to search for others we recognize as our own. So we get roman-tically attached to fictional characters, or romantically attach one fictional character to another and ship them. We chase straight girls. We date someone, dump them because we're afraid of our own feelings, then miss them until the day we die. The ex-girlfriends of our ex-girlfriends are our girlfriends. As annoying, lonely, desperate, isolating, and pathetic as this freestyle longing can feel, it also means each act of desire builds a new queer world, baby. In the words of Fever Ray: "Every time we fuck, we win."

So then, to answer your question ("Am I foolish for feeling this way?") with another question: What is more straight-up valid and gorgeously queer than two human beings falling in love with each other's online simulacra unimpeded by physical space? Nothing.

Next round: Are you foolish for believing J is your soulmate, and that "she's supposed to be in your life?"

Hmm. Come, take this mug of mint tea. Over there, do you see my walnut Anecdote dresser? Top drawer? Yes, get that book and hand it to me. Ah, my embossed leather album of life mistakes. Here's a good page. Ah yes, the girl I'll call FMK, because over the years we spent either dating furiously or not talking, I felt like doing all three at once, all the time. Fuck, marry, kill. A full-corn cargo-shorts bleach-blonde futch who stepped out of OkCupid. We used to finish each other's sentences too.

Even though the only activities on our private Scissor Island were fucking, crying, drinking, and two-person poetry readings, I was struck down. She was the one for me, truly and verily, the psychic detective of my secret self, my awe-inspiring puzzle: How can it feel as if I have known her since birth yet everything about her is new? In serious, die-holding-hands, big, long-haul love. The greatest, wildest miracle was that it was that way for her too, vicey-versey.

We clocked three months and then she ice cold dumped me, for the same girl she had dumped for me before. It was like being every character in Robyn's "Call Your Girlfriend." A great song, but you don't want to live there.

I angrily obsessed at each increasing interval of her wholesale disappearance: one day, two days, a week, a month, a year, two years of silence. Why, why, why? I constantly sought out more information for my theories.

One night I felt a rush of Yes Today Satan and went for it: opened a chat window. Hi. FMK responds? And she's wondering how I am? And she's really missed me? And I'm not wondering why, if she missed me, she'd wait for me to initiate conversation? We're going to hang out just for closure. We're going to hang out again, but we're not going to do anything. We hung out again and did . . . everything . . . oh god, it's the same, she's the same. So we both dumped our other girl-friends for a victorious reunion, where we would know the value of what we lost and regained and FINALLY be TOGETHER.

That second round was fanfic for the original: less nuanced, more sentimental, more pornographic, and shorter. We made it one and a half months and then she flash-dumped me, again (for a different girl this time, thank god).

Years after we stopped dating, I sent FMK a relevant part of my diary from that time—no, I don't know why I did it, and yes, I know something is wrong with me. She returned a piping-hot personal pan pizza of extremely right-on critique: that I talked about her like she was a demon or a monster, a small jagged piece of mirror for me, less than a person. All that bullshit and she didn't even need to be there for it. My love wasn't what I thought it was, either.

You can put this back in the drawer, dear. As you can see, J is giving me FMK vibes. The subjective experience of another's feelings and thoughts are permanently mysterious because we each exist as a divided independent conscious-ness. All relationships are long-distance relationships; those also separated by geog-raphy simply explicitly so.

When you write that you had to make sure J writing you "wasn't yet another dream [you were] having about her"? When the real and dream versions of a person act indistinguishably, that's a warning. Like a dream, there are some big plot holes here: For instance, a greeting of "holy shit" after a long separation is typically reserved for the person who didn't ghost. Why'd she go away the first time?

Her eternal return is a function of something inside you she's representing. J's absence didn't create it, and the future together that you imagine wouldn't fix it. Lucinda adds: "Because she is literally projected material made in your own head, she will always be your kryptonite." Your desire for her is all-consuming and endlessly interesting because it's not her that will satisfy it. A recurring dream always has the same ending. There's no way to prevent what's coming except to wake up. We deserve better and so do the people we love.

Whatever happens with J, these feelings are jewels of self-knowledge, shaped like skulls, *sparkling and sparkling.* Cease-less, and 100 percent yours, baby. You write: "Whatever it is about J, my heart refuses to let go of her." Maybe "whatever" is in how you felt after your child-hood BFF left you? How you "put on a brave face" in heart-break or "put up walls" with your exes? Don't be embarrassed if the answers are simple. (Mine were all about my mom!) Simple is rarely easy. And don't get tripped up by J's pretty reflec-tion. Grab the jewels with both hands and run. ❤

Love and other signs of system collapse,

—LOLA PELLEGRINO
Writer & Guest Expert

SUPPORT SYSTEMS

FRIENDSHIP & QUEER COMMUNITY

CHAPTER FOUR

A while back, I wrote a lesbian advice column for a small web magazine called *Argot*. The column came out every other week, and I struggled to meet deadlines. I'm a slow writer, and giving advice doesn't come naturally to me. My tone would be sympathetic one column and snarky the next. And, like anything written for the internet, I could gauge reactions as soon as the column posted. People loved when I dissected a particularly selfish question or prescribed self-reflection. There's so little justice when it comes to love crimes, I think, that there's a real satisfaction in reading a low-stakes takedown. Unsurprisingly, columns where I was affirming and nice received less praise.

Someone once asked me: Do you ever feel like the person asking for advice is lying and just trying to get published? And the truth is, only once or twice! The majority of the questions I receive are self-reflective and thoughtful. I can tell the author is trying to be impartial and see beyond themselves. At the same time, every question is just a snapshot of a relationship, situation, or life. It's written at a time of stress or existential crisis. Some questions are hundreds of words long, others are just a few sentences. At their most basic core, however, all these questions are asking the same thing: How can I better love myself and others?

 **I recently started identifying** as lesbian after describing myself as bisexual for as long as I can remember. In many ways, this has felt like finding myself, but I still have a lot of lingering guilt and regret about my past sexual experiences with men. At the moment, I have this sexually inexperienced male friend who I know is into me. He knows about my sexual past, which involved sleeping around with a fair number of men. With hindsight most of those experiences were extremely negative—half an attempt at self-conversion therapy and half feeling as though I owed it to men to please them sexually. Although the feelings of not wanting to be a lesbian are gone, the feeling of owing something sexually to men is not—especially with this male friend. He is often doing me favors, such as letting me crash at his place or helping me with university work, and other people who know us both have jokingly told me I am "using him" for these things because he perhaps expects something in return, knowing my sexual past and thinking I still identify as bisexual. I am starting to feel really guilty about this and wonder if I do owe him in return for his friendship, even though our friendship is ultimately the same as any of my others besides his "being into me." How do I stop feeling like I owe something to men who show me friendship?

—MAURA, 19

A. Your friend is an adult man with free will. He's making a conscious, informed decision each and every time he lets you sleep over or helps you with your work—things that are, by the way, normal things friends do for friends. No matter who you've slept with in the past, you're not obligated to have sex with him to reciprocate his friendship. The truth is that your friend could pay off all your student loans or jump into shark-infested water to save your life, and you still wouldn't be obligated to have sex with him. He could be dying of cancer and his last, dying wish could be to lose his virginity to you, and you still would not be mean or unreasonable for saying no. You don't owe him, or anyone, sex.

It sounds like you understand this on a logical level, but emotionally you're struggling to establish boundaries for yourself and break out of a pattern that's making you miserable. You've already taken the first step, which is recognizing the problem: You have sex with men

because you feel obligated to and you want to punish yourself for being a lesbian. Afterward, you shame spiral because you had sex that you didn't really want. It might help to take a break from sex completely until you're in a place where you can consent in a way that feels authentic and enthusiastic. Your question doesn't say anything about drinking or drugs, but sometimes it can help to think about the substances, friends, and situations that enable self-destructive behavior.

You are not a bad lesbian because you've had sex with men. Yes, there are lesbians who have known they were gay from earliest age. But there are many, many lesbians who, like you, figured it out after trying to make it work with men. I know lesbians who used to be married to men and thought of themselves as straight, some-times for decades. When you're a woman, the whole world tells you to love men and organize your life around securing their attention and validation. The poet Adrienne Rich called this "compulsory heterosexuality" and it's worth a Google. Women aren't taught to follow their desires or have sex for their own gratification and pleasure. Like, I was constantly having horny thoughts as a kid and teenager, but I didn't start masturbating until after I started having part-nered sex. It just didn't occur to me that I could get myself off, so I didn't try.

Find some lesbian and queer friends. If your university has an LGBTQIA+ center, see if they offer therapy or support groups. Take a gender studies class while you're at it. When you meet other lesbians, you'll realize that your own experiences and feel-ings are pretty normal.

Also, I also came out when I was nineteen. At the time, I felt so old! Like you, I thought that everyone had themselves figured out. When really, there's no magical age when everyone has their lives and sexualities pinned down.

Something I sense from your question is that you're afraid of disappointing others and being disliked. When you sacrifice your own wishes to make someone else happy, you just end up miserable. Sometimes when other people call us mean or a bitch or a dyke, it's a sign that we are alive and out in the world, making our own decisions. Saying "no" can also be a litmus test for the people in our lives. If it turns out that your friend was only nice to you because he was hoping to score, then you're better off without him. ♥

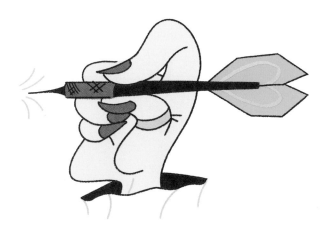

I'm just getting out of a yearlong relationship with a girl I love and loved very much, which sucks. Our breakup was stereotypically dykey in that we both reiterated the realness of what we had and our gratitude to each other for having been there through hard times. She apologized for hurting me and validated my feelings—all really, really good things. We're planning to take a break from talking for as long as I need and then eventually to try becoming friends. Again, classic, and really reassuring to me as I enter grieving. But the PROBLEM is, so much of what I've absorbed about how to deal with heartbreak revolves around learning to see the flaws in your former partner and resenting their missteps, something I'd rather not force myself to do. Is there a way to separate but still remain compassionate toward her, or can I never get the distance I need to move on without cultivating at least some dislike or distrust?

—LIRA, 22

A. I thought about this question for a long time. I kept opening the Word doc and closing it without writing anything. A lot of the questions that come across my desk are from people who can't stop obsessing about their ex or move past a breakup—people who don't even recognize themselves because they're swimming in post-breakup jealousy, anger, and resentment. I always respond by saying that you're not a bad person for feeling like garbage after a breakup. You're a lesbian, not a saint. It takes time to recover from heartbreak, much more time than people are usually willing to give themselves. In my experience, the old adage that it takes half the time of the relationship to get over the relationship holds true. It doesn't mean I'm crying in public or unable to date new people, just that I might feel bruised. I might feel anxious before going somewhere where there's a high probability of running into my ex, or I might have a bad day for totally unrelated reasons and go through my ex's new girlfriend's Instagram to make myself feel even worse. Healthy!

If I'm hearing you correctly, it sounds like you don't harbor any anger toward your ex. You're looking for that extra oomph to move on with your life. Injecting your daily routine with voluntary, low-stakes change—taking a trip, getting a daring new haircut, rearranging your room, or exploring a new hobby like gardening or kayaking—will help you embrace change in your love life.

Your question also brings up some concerns about becoming friends with your ex. In my experience, the stereotype that lesbians stay friends with their exes is accurate. A lot of my straight friends, on the other hand, regard relationships as failures if they don't end in marriage. There's a sense that one person is the winner and the other person is the loser. My lesbian friends are more like, "We're just on different journeys" and "We're better off as friends." In the majority of my breakups, I can see past my hurt feelings and recognize that my ex is a complicated human who exists outside of her relationship to me. That's not to say the transition from partners to friends is easy for lesbians. It takes communication, intention,

and a lot of work. In some cases, it takes a long time for the pain and disappointment of a breakup to dissipate. I've definitely ended relationships with zero interest in friendship, only to change my mind a year later.

I give you permission to feel bitter and bruised. If it gives you some cheap joy, complain about your ex to a friend you trust, someone who understands that you're just being petty. But if you genuinely don't feel any regret or anger, try establishing some boundaries and distance. Ask each other: How will your friendship be different from your girlfriendship? The last thing you want is to rush into friendship with no intention or boundaries—the lines will get real blurred, real fast. Agree to take a month off from talking to each other on any platform; when it's over, you can check in to see if you're both feeling ready to start building a friendship. ♥

When I was in high school, I spent countless nights wide awake, distressed over how to identify my sexuality. I almost came to a conclusion, and then was asked out by a very shy boy, who became my one and only high school boyfriend for a year and a half. Once that ended, the worry returned, but this time, with resolution: I was clearly attracted to women, nearly exclusively, and I was a lesbian. I accepted this with time and began coming out to friends and family. All was well. Fall 2016, I started my freshman year of college at a Christian college with a heavily homophobic environment, something I was unaware of before enrolling. I decided to be open about my sexuality regardless, and be vocal about issues that affected the LGBT community. This certainly took an emotional toll on me; I lost friends once they discovered my sexuality and often felt ostracized both in and outside of the classroom. I wasn't aware of how much it affected me, however, until I eventually withdrew from the school halfway through my sophomore year. I was truly alone; I was removed from the small queer community that I had found in college, and, being back home, I had no friends locally to reach out to. My parents didn't make much of an effort to understand how I felt, either. So I was very alone, and as a result I turned to dating apps, because I was longing for emotional connections. I'm from a small, rural town in the Midwest, with very few queer women in the area. So I started talking to men out of convenience, and a lot of them. At first it was a new boy every month, and then it became a new boy every one to two weeks, one semi-long-term boyfriend, and then multiple men each week for short periods of time. This went on for almost a year, until I was so furious with the lack of emotional intelligence and accountability I was finding in these men that I stopped having sex, period. The thing is, Maddy, I don't know what I want anymore. Well, no, I do: I want a relationship with another woman. The problem is, I'm afraid to seek it out. I'm afraid of finding other queer people in my current city, I'm afraid of pursuing women, I'm afraid of being rejected by women. But most of all, I'm afraid that I've become so bitter and cold from the horrid encounters I've had with men that I won't be able to love someone the way they deserve to be loved. And I don't think that burning myself out by being proudly out in a hateful community has aided me much, either. If anything, I think it's also contributing to preventing me from surrounding myself with queer love and people again. I know that ultimately I need to go back to therapy and be single for a while in order to date health-ily again, so I'm not going to burden you with the question of what I need to do in order to fix this. What I want to know from you is, What are some small steps I can take toward finding a community in my area? What can I do to help myself feel more comfortable about my sexuality? Does not having any queer friends or a queer community do me harm, even if I am afraid of losing them again?

—CHRISTINE, 21

A. I'm sorry that Christian college was a trauma factory. I'm sorry for the isolation you felt in your hometown, and that the men you dated were unkind. You've survived so much, Christine. I can tell from this question that you understand exactly what you're feeling and how you got here. The past few years have taught you that it's better to be alone than with someone who makes you feel smaller, and that it's better to have no community than one that's hateful and homophobic. Right now, it might feel like all you know is how to be alone. When, really, knowing how to be alone

is an amazing asset as you begin to make friends and date again. It means you won't settle for people who treat you poorly.

You feel alienated from your queerness, which makes sense because you never got to experience the fun parts of being queer. When you were in high school, defining your sexuality was a major source of anxiety. In college, your lesbian pride made you a pariah. Now that you're in a new city, you can finally define queerness on your own terms.

When you ask how to feel more comfortable with your

queerness, my first instinct is to talk about queer community. When I say queer community, I mean a source of love and care that's beyond friendship. I mean people who can reflect your experiences back at you and who understand what it's like to experience homophobia and alienation in a way that your straight friends and family of origin might not. I love being in lesbian households and being around lesbian energy. It's like coffee to me, that's the only way I can describe it— comforting and necessary. At the same time, there's a lot of danger in assuming that lesbian and queer people are inherently good or kind. Queer communities and relationships can be toxic and abusive. Every single person, no matter how gay, is capable of making mistakes and causing harm.

I don't say all this to scare you, just to underscore that even the best relationships can be sources of conflict and pain. Other humans will hurt and disappoint you. The solution is not to isolate yourself and distrust everyone, but rather to let your gut and hard-won wisdom guide you. Do a lot of journaling. Go to therapy. Adopt a pet. Make some friends (see pages 28–30 and 102–105 for specific tips on how to find queer friends). Remind yourself that Christian college and your hometown are in the past. This next chapter of your life is all about queer joy. ♥

I'm kind of in a weird place in my life and unsure whether I should be settling into a life of normalcy or traveling the world. Do I stay with this girl I've been comfortable with for over a year now (bed death and all) and retire to the hills with our cat and dog menagerie? Or do I totally break it off and start a new life in a new city and get interwoven into a queer poly family? It's so hard to tell if I'm missing out or just getting restless since I'm twenty-five and drastically "behind" in relationships and worldly experiences. It's so hard to tell whether my life totally sucks, and I would love an outsider's opinion! I don't wanna have dyke FOMO, but all the same I feel a sense of jealousy hearing about everyone else living life, and I feel quite small at times.

—SPONGE, 25

A. It's unfair to compare your actual life and relationship to your dream polycule. It's also unfair—to both you *and* your girlfriend—for you to stay in a relationship that you view as boring and second-rate.

When you say you feel jealous of everyone else's life, are you talking about people you know personally or internet people? Instagram is not the truth. Most people project a distorted, cherry-picked narrative of their lives and relationships. I, personally, have made gooey posts about relationships and partners I was not invested in at all. Also, some of the loneliest, brokest times in my life have been after I moved to a new city. Even in instances where I knew a few people going in and was actively trying to make new friends, it took me a while to feel settled. It takes a long time to build a chosen family, especially if you're also looking for work and adjusting to a new place.

Only you can determine whether or not your life "totally sucks." You can honor your feelings of dissatisfaction and boredom and even take action, while also acknowledging that the grass will always seem gayer somewhere else. 💜

Q. I recently went through a tough breakup with a queer social butterfly, and I stopped going out for a while so that I could heal without having to see her at every event. But now that I'm feeling better and trying to rebuild my social life, I get really intense social anxiety wherever I go. When I'm around queer people, I'm anxious about being cool and detached and hot enough. When I'm around straight people or in a mixed group, I'm anxious about being "too gay" or about taking up too much space. I overthink all my interactions and get too tongue-tied to talk to anyone. Then I end up the burdensome wallflower standing in the corner by herself. I WANT to navigate these social settings with ease and confidence, but even though I know I'm a kind and interesting person, I can't bring that out in me when I'm around people I don't know very well. I feel foolish trying to fake it. How do I let my personality shine through and connect to people?

—RILEY, 24

A. It takes guts to go to parties by yourself and talk to new people. It's so vulnerable! Whenever I feel self-conscious or intimidated by a room full of strangers, I remind myself that everyone is wrapped up in their own insecurities, drama, and social circles. It's kind of like when you went to parties with your social butterfly ex-girlfriend—you probably weren't looking around or wondering how you could connect with the people sitting alone at the bar. Now that you are a person alone at the bar, you're like, *This is hard!* Maybe you'll be inspired to reach out to someone new.

There's a stereotype that queer women don't talk to each other, they just stare and ache with longing. I have talked myself out of approaching hot, interesting people hundreds of times. I didn't want to come across as creepy or pushy, which is

actually ridiculous because I probably would've just been like, "Hi." I've also tried talking to people and been rudely dismissed. Sometimes these people were actual jerks. But most of the time, they were visibly terrified. It's a skill to be receptive to meeting new people, just like it's a skill to walk up to someone new and start a conversation. The internet has us all out of practice.

If you're at a house party, it can help to give yourself a job. Ask the host if you can bartend—this way you're still at the party, but there's no pressure to talk or act a certain way. One of my ex-girlfriends volunteers at a queer archive because she meets so many new people tabling at community events. Anything that feels grounding, even if it's just reminding yourself that you belong in the space, will help with your social anxiety.

You must also accept that as a queer person, you will be invited to some of the most awkward and psychically draining parties known to earth. I recently attended a film screening that featured food and concessions. This film was three hours long and afterward, the hosts made us all stand in line to wash our own individual dishes. One time I went to a lesbian dinner party where a couple was fighting with such intensity and tunnel vision that everyone crept away to drink on the porch. There's nothing you can do in these situations, except get through them.

And finally, I felt a lot of FOMO and pressure to go out in my early twenties. Now if I stay out past midnight, I start to miss my dog. Straight bars and big anonymous dance parties make me feel anxious, so I'll ask my friends if I can join them for brunch the next morning instead. There are so many ways to be out in the world; I don't need to force myself to go anywhere that feels like a job. ♥

I'm a young lesbian, and I feel like my social life is falling apart. About a year ago, I moved to a new city and tried to keep in contact with my friends from home. But, as months went on, everyone seemed less and less interested in keeping in contact with me. The few friendships I've made since I've moved still feel budding and fragile. In addition to this, I recently had a really bad, irreconcilable falling out with the girl who was my first girlfriend, and even though we'd been broken up for years, I never really got over her. During the past year, I've made several attempts at dating that left me feeling insecure and defeated. I've been wallowing for weeks, and I feel like I don't have anyone to lean on or to offer me emotional support. Most of my dissatisfaction with my relationships comes from feeling like I'm the only one putting effort toward maintaining them. How can I cope with this? How can I rebuild a support system in my life? How can I fully move on from the people who aren't in my life anymore?

—BENNIE, 18

GUEST EXPERT • **ELLEN KEMPNER**

A. Hi! This is so real and almost exactly something that I went through once. My first girlfriend dumped me minutes after I got back from my first-ever tour, and I thought I'd never heal. In my wallowing, I dropped out of school and moved to Boston to live with my best friend, who needed a roommate. Something I didn't take into account, however, was that my best friend was constantly touring, meaning I was alone most of the time. I got so lonely, I adopted some guinea pigs to help ease my mind. Attempts at dating were all fruitless (partly due to the guinea pigs—they were always squealing and kicking shit all over my room, which was NOT sexy at ALL) and led to me feeling more and more defeated and hopeless. That hopelessness definitely infiltrated my desire to make friends as well.

It took a lot of work to get through this period, but it was one of the greatest learning experiences of my life. The first thing I have to emphasize is that finding a queer community— not a queer lover, but a group of queer friends—is CRUCIAL when moving to a new city while gay. As a musician, I found my community by going to a lot of DIY shows in my neighborhood and finding bands that I liked and wanted to support. I don't know what city you moved to, but I can assure you that a queer music scene exists there somewhere! You definitely don't need to be a musician to fit

into that community either; a lot of the friends I made in that scene didn't play music, they just enjoyed and supported it. Like me, they wanted to find more queer people to surround themselves with. It's scary and intimidating at first, but honestly, everyone in a social setting is projecting a version of themselves that they think will make them liked and respected, and everyone is just as scared and insecure as you are, even if they're already deeply ingrained in a scene. Unfortunately, as the newbie, you're probably going to be the one in the position of starting up conversations, so just keep that in mind when you're approaching people. Remember that being the new kid can be fun! People want new

friends and will be excited to meet you!

That being said, I have to address what you said about feeling like you're the only person maintaining your relationships. That state of mind is the killer; it will do you no good. It can be disappointing when people don't pull their weight, but it doesn't always mean that they care less. Some people just don't socialize the same way you do; maybe they get anxious about saying the right thing when they see your texts, maybe they know you're in transition right now and don't want to interrupt that for you, maybe they're so busy they don't have the brain space to make plans! There are so many reasons for

people not initiating plans and conversations that don't have to do with them not wanting to hang with you. This may sound tough, but you have to stop keeping track of who texted first, who invited first, because it's really so futile. If you want to hang out with someone, you have to put the work in. Don't let their different social skills let you down or make you doubt them. This is not to say that you should let people walk over you, though. If you find yourself reaching out to someone and they're not making time for you, it's not worth it. But if you're the one reaching out, and that person is always down to hang out, and when you do hang out, they make you feel good, that's really all that matters.

Keep this in mind when it comes to your fear that the friendships you have right now seem "budding and fragile." I think you're underestimating how resilient new friendships can be! Fretting over them being destroyed will take a lot of the fun out of it, and (I know this sounds super corny) that's what finding friends should be about: having fun. When I first moved to Boston I made the mistake of treating new friends as people to be sort of . . . collected? Like to prove to myself that I was gonna be okay. The people that I put too many expectations on in that way ended up becoming distant acquaintances at best. After thinking a lot about why I was treating my social life like a stack of Pokémon cards, I came to the conclusion that my breakup really fucked me up! A romantic breakup can affect how you act as a friend too, not just as a lover. Breakups make people desperate for the validation that they can be loved. It sounds like a lot of your fears about ruining new friendships could be stemming from anxieties you have about dating.

This applies to how you view your old friendships as well. Your feeling that your old friends are growing less and less interested in you is, no offense, probably just your own shit projected onto those relationships. Remember that you're the one who moved away, so your old friends could very well think the same thing about you. You need to be honest with them about how you feel and not treat them like they're exes. Don't try to "fully move on" from them in the way that you are with your ex-girlfriend. They're not the same! Just because you moved cities doesn't mean you have to recycle your entire social life. In fact, reconciling with old friends will probably make it way easier to make new friends. It'll help alleviate the pressure you're putting on yourself and remind you of what it feels like to be yourself with people you love.

You're in transition right now, and that's never easy. This time can feel endless and hopeless, but it's really all about finding a balance. A balance between old and new friends, a balance between expectations and trusting the unknown. You may not feel like you have emotional support or someone to lean on right now, and that's really hard, but you will get there. This is a new phase in your life, but it's not a completely new life. You're still the same person; the experiences and people you've known are what make you you, so don't leave them behind for the sake of finding a new support system. ♥

—ELLEN KEMPNER
Musician & Guest Expert

 **How can trans women** survive in the queer community when we know our inclusion is always for the sake of making a dyke event look progressive? How can our friendships survive when only other trans women care about our material well-being in a dependable way? When we're all exhausted trying to care for each other, how do we care for others? How do we keep ourselves from becoming bitter at the many ways other queers turn away from our needs? How do we generate kindness in ourselves when even this world we try to create remains so hostile to us after years laboring for our own needs?

—ASHER, 30

GUEST EXPERT • MEY RUDE

A. I think there are going to be quite a few readers who will read your question and automatically reject your premise outright. They want to believe that the queer community is better than that, and that we're creating safe spaces for trans women to not just live, but thrive. Even I want to believe that. But, in reality, you're right. It's exhausting and depressing to be a trans person in public, and unfortunately, it's often worse in queer spaces.

It's been in queer communities where I've felt most self-conscious about my physical size as a trans woman. It's been in queer communities where I've felt afraid to flirt. It's in queer communities where I felt like nothing I ever did mattered.

Most of the work of changing that actually needs to be done by AFAB queer people. They need to actively practice unlearning transmisogyny. They need to go out and make friends with the trans women in their communities. They need to educate themselves and challenge transphobia and gender essentialism when they see it. They're the ones who need to not just punch TERFs, but if there's a TERF in their family or friend group, we need them to talk to that person and change their mind. This is especially true of people who already consider themselves trans allies. We need y'all to use that cis privilege and any pull in the queer community that you have to make queer spaces better for trans women.

Asher, you asked what trans women can do, though, so the first thing I want to say is that if you can afford it and

have access to trans-affirming healthcare, go to therapy. If you can find a queer or trans therapist, that's ideal, but that's also difficult in most places. The best way to be a healthy person in a world that is harmful to you is to go to therapy.

But even if therapy is not available to you right now, there are some things you can do. You have some tools to help you in this fight.

How can we not only survive in queer communities, but also develop lasting and deep friendships with the people there? Travel in packs. Try to find at least one other trans woman near you that you like, and make friends with her. Go to queer events together, bring more trans friends if you can find them. If there are a bunch of us there, then none of us can be the token trans woman.

Another important thing you can do is to not give up on those queer communities. We've got to keep moving closer to the future that we want to live in.

TERFs want us out of queer spaces, so let's do the opposite. A friend once told me, "We need more trans women in the world, not fewer of us," and I think about that every day. The world is better with more of us in it, and queer spaces and communities are too.

I know it's hard to keep on going when you've had so much bad luck finding real friends, but I promise, queer spaces are getting better. There are plenty of people whose welcoming of trans women is only surface level (if that), but there are also plenty of people who really do mean what they say. And those people are working hard to make things better for us in queer spaces. Find them and hold them close.

How do we care for others when we're so exhausted ourselves? Again, I turn to relationships with other trans people. I find spending time with other trans women relaxes me deep in my soul in a way that nothing else does. Even if it's just in a group chat or on social media, seeing a bunch of other trans women

living their lives and talking about mundane, relatable things energizes and heals me.

Talk about your feelings. Communicate. Believe the best of people, and remind yourself that your friends love you. Establish and respect boundaries, but also tell each other how you feel. The way to process and grow from feelings is to talk about them.

One of the ways I stop myself from becoming bitter about all my negative experiences in queer communities is to look at trans women being happy. Look at trans kids, look at trans elders, look at how happy you were in the moments where you felt gender euphoria. Think about those things often. Talk about them, try to make them happen more often.

Volunteer with kids if that's something in your wheelhouse. Working with queer youth always gives me so much hope for the future. When you meet a nine-year-old who's already figured out her gender, you can't help but realize that children are geniuses who are going to save the world.

Tell your friends you love them. Try to see them once a week or more. Set up group texts. Tell yourself you love you. When things are nice, say out loud that they're nice. Later, think back on your memories of those nice things when you're in bed, or in the shower, or on the toilet. Tell yourself that you love yourself.

How do we generate kindness in ourselves? That's the hardest question of them all. One thing that helped me a lot was repeating affirmations. For over a year I had a set of affirmations I wrote as my phone wallpaper, so that every time I looked at my phone, I'd read them. Here's what I wrote; you can come up with your own:

TAKE A BREATH. BREATHE IN FOR 4 SECONDS. HOLD IT FOR 7. RELEASE IT FOR 4.

THIS IS TEMPORARY, PEOPLE LOVE YOU.

LIVE FOR YOURSELF.

ASSUME GOOD INTENTIONS AND GIVE THE BENEFIT OF THE DOUBT.

THINGS WILL HAPPEN WHEN THE TIME IS RIGHT. THERE'S NO STANDARD ON WHAT THAT TIMING SHOULD BE. SO CHIN UP, LOVE YOURSELF FIRST.

I still remind myself every day that everyone's timing is different, that everyone's life happens at its own pace. Waiting is hard, but it's worth it. I tell myself every day that the future is bigger than the past.

I also remind myself that most people are good; they're trying, and they're working on getting better. When I assume the best in people, I'm very often proven right.

Most importantly, I remember that I'm one of those people too. I'm good, and I'm trying, and I'm working on being better. I deserve the benefit of the doubt. I deserve kindness and love, and even when no one else in the world will give me those things, I can still show them to myself. ♥

—MEY RUDE
Writer, Consultant & Guest Expert

LETTING YOURSELF BE KNOWN

COMING OUT & FAMILIES OF ORIGIN

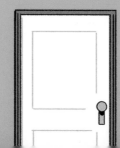

CHAPTER FIVE

I started keeping a journal when I was twenty-one. I had just graduated from college and moved to Portland, OR. I had no money and no plan, just a vague sense that Portland was cool and if I lived there, my life would be cool by proxy. Instead, I spent my first weeks desperately looking for work and crying on public transportation. I finally found a job at a group home for disabled adults. My bus commute was an hour each way, and I would write in an old notebook to pass the time. I didn't start recording my thoughts and feelings with any kind of intention, however, until I reread an old entry and realized that I'd completely forgotten that day. I didn't remember shopping for bras at Target or worrying that my best friend was ignoring my texts, and I definitely didn't remember feeling miserable and hopeless. After that, journaling became an essential part of how I process and reflect on my life. I try to write a few paragraphs every day. Recently, I was reading through an old journal and I kept seeing a name I didn't recognize. This person seemed like a real louse, but I couldn't, for a million dollars, remember who she was. I finally found some context clues and BOOM, I remembered—the object of my ire was an old manager at a job that I'd worked at for a few semesters in grad school. This woman would monitor every second of my shift, then pressure me to subscribe to wine delivery apps with her referral code. I felt so strongly about my manager at the time, but I'd totally forgotten her a short while later.

Kelsey and I got the same surreal feeling reading through many of the questions in this book. We realized that we had forgotten what it really feels like to be in the closet. We'd forgotten how lying, even when it's your only option, is accompanied by a pressure that builds in your chest and feels a little like guilt. We no longer remembered how exhausting it is to be out to your friends and the internet but not your family of origin. The submissions for this book brought those feelings back in a way that felt meaningful and cathartic. I think this is one of the magical things about a project like *The Ex-Girlfriend of My Ex-Girlfriend Is My Girlfriend*—even if you don't share someone's exact experiences, maybe you'll see your own life and feelings reflected back at you.

I've always had an odd relationship with my mother—with my whole family, really; we're from Texas, and they're all very Republican. Don't get me wrong, my parents are good people. They are accepting people, or at least they say so. And they do say so, dropping the classic lines "We know plenty of people like that"; "We work with people from all backgrounds and don't judge"; and my favorite, "We don't have a problem with gay people, we just don't want it shoved in our face." For the longest time I was so sure and confident I was straight, until my senior year of high school, when I started secretly dating my then best friend, "K." It was an amazing summer spent with her. We went on each of our family vacations together, celebrated Fourth of July, had our first kisses together, and in the end it didn't last. Now I'm in my junior year of college, single, happy, and very, very bi! But I'm not out to my family, and I don't have plans to come out to them anytime soon. As I get older I'm finding more and more things they say and do to be offensive toward LGBTQ people. Disguised, of course, with the statements I mentioned earlier. It's very difficult to defend the people in my community, my friends from college, and myself to my family without having to come out and say it to them! That the people they're putting down and calling "others" includes me. I don't truly think my parents are homophobic, but they come from a different generation, with different values, and that makes them who they are. I shouldn't have to come out to my family to prove a point. I don't know how to be happy with who I am, how to defend myself to them, without being out.

—MADISON, 20

A. Homofobia can manifest in many forms and frequencies. Your parents' comments are hurtful and corrosive to your self-esteem. When you try to talk to them, they deny responsibility and refuse to see the impact of their words. That's not okay. Your parents may be old and from Texas, but that doesn't mean they get a pass on evolving and being decent humans.

Something that the queer people in my life say all the time that also rings true from my own experience is that it can be really, really difficult to predict how parents will react when their children come out. There are conservative parents who are immediately accepting and liberal parents who lose their shit. There are parents who react poorly at first but grow into acceptance and fearless allyship with time. Sometimes one parent is on board, and the other parent is not. I know my dad accepts me, but it's like an unspoken understanding that we share. We've never directly discussed my queerness and

we probably never will. It's possible that, after you come out, your parents will *still* make homophobic comments—only their excuses will be like, and I'm just riffing here, "You're one of the normal ones" or, "It doesn't matter that you're bisexual. You'll marry a man someday." Sadly, having a queer child is no guarantee that parents will evolve and work through their homophobia.

So what can you do? Remember that when you engage your parents and ask them to reconsider their oppressive beliefs, you're doing difficult and demanding work. Nothing you say or do will prompt them to change if they refuse to do so. It's not your responsibility to help them become better people. It is, however, your responsibility to keep yourself safe and healthy. You're allowed to spend less time with your parents or leave situations that make you feel like less of a person.

To be honest, the final line of your question—"I don't know

how to be happy with who I am, how to defend myself to them, without being out"— is a pretty compelling reason to come out. Still, it is complicated. I get it. The decision to stay closeted is also complicated. You know yourself and your life better than anyone. The only thing I would say for certain is if you're relying on your parents' financial support to attend college and there's a chance they might withdraw that support, or you think they might react violently, please don't come out until you're financially independent. Go into that conversation with your eyes open, and make sure you have a strong support network of people who love and accept you. ♥

Q. I'm **AFAB,** I've only come out to myself fairly recently, and I'm like, still fighting not to feel guilty for wanting to fuck girls. I know it's ridiculous, but I'm so hyperwary of, like, re-creating the male gaze that I feel like a cartoon wolf version of Hugh Hefner every time I peep some under-boob. How do I get over the feeling of being an objectifying creep and start kissing girls, lol?

—JORDAN, 26

A. This question and variations of it come across my desk all the time. There are so many negative stereotypes and lies about queer people in mainstream culture. We soak up these messages as children, and they become encoded in our self-image. It's difficult to express your attraction and desire when you've been conditioned to see yourself as predatory, sinful, or disgusting. Another term for this phenomenon is "internalized homophobia." The clearest path to self-acceptance is to surround yourself with queer community and media. And, of course, therapy can be an invaluable tool when confronting shame. This might be a Tumblr throwback, but I find a lot of comfort in the words often attributed to Anaïs Nin: "Shame is the lie someone told you about yourself."

You're not a bad person because you saw some under-boob and it gave you feelings. Finding women hot and wanting to fuck them is not the same as harassing them. If you approached the underboob-haver and she was like, "No thanks, I'm not interested," I doubt you'd continue to pursue her or make her feel unsafe for saying no. You would not catcall her or follow her home making kissy noises. You would not send her unwanted sexts. You'd take the message and respect her wishes, crossing zero boundaries along the way. The truth is that if you're worried about being a creep, you're probably not a creep. ♥

My friend recently came out to me as a trans-feminine person. Generally, she is still closeted, and no one knows but close friends and family. Her reason is that she is worried about getting fired from her job as a programmer and UIX designer, and losing her income and connections. What do you do if a friend comes out to you, but they are not out to the world? How can I support her gender identity and transition despite this?

A. Your friend came out to you because she trusts you and wants you in her life. And you clearly care a lot about her happiness and well-being, or else you wouldn't be writing this question. Sometimes, as cis people with good intentions, we overthink things and stress ourselves out when it comes to showing up for our trans friends. Let your friend know you love and support her. Ask how you can be there for her. It's possible she wants help with something specific, but most likely, she just needs you to be there for her. ♥

I am a lesbian and my younger sister is bisexual. I recently came out to my parents and it was really difficult. My mom came around to it eventually and has since met my girlfriend, but my dad is basically ignoring me. Whenever he does talk to me, it's never about my identity or my relationship. I constantly worry about my relationship with my girlfriend progressing while my relationship with my dad deteriorates. My sister is not out to our parents and has no plans to come out to them. My question is, is it bad that sometimes I feel a little resentful that she can freely live her queer life while I am always worrying about mine? She has rainbow stuff everywhere and has even gone on an international trip to visit a girlfriend, but my parents don't even question it. They assume she is straight, and she doesn't correct them. Every time I think this I feel extremely biphobic. I have a great relationship with my sister, so this isn't something I want to talk to her about for fear that she would be angry or upset. I obviously would never push her to come out if she didn't want to, but it still makes me resentful that she gets the freedom of being comfortable in her identity without the burden of homophobic parents.

—ELIZA, 24

A. You are not a bad person for having messy, negative feelings toward your sister. Everyone feels jealous and resentful sometimes, especially when life gets overwhelming and difficult. It's when we allow negative feelings to cloud our relationships or when we presume to know the exact contours of someone else's life that problems arise.

To be honest, Eliza, I'm amazed you haven't already spilled your guts and told her exactly how you're feeling. I have three older brothers and the defining aspect of our sibling relationship is brutal, unmitigated honesty. I'm amazed by your perspective. Not only do you understand that you and your sister are different people with different priorities, but you also respect her autonomy and privacy.

Your sister doesn't have to come out to your parents, but there are other ways she can support you and show solidarity during this difficult time. Maybe she could talk to your dad about why he's being so cold. Maybe you two can make a pact where like, if things at the dinner table veer into hurtful and homophobic territory, you both get up and leave. As the "straight" daughter, she could guide your parents to counseling or PFLAG resources. I don't know the specific dynamics of your family, but at the very least she could step up and be a warm, comforting presence when your parents are being jerks. Give your sister a chance to show up for you! Tell her how she can support you during this difficult time. Another reason why you need to talk to your sister is that you two have so much to commiserate about! This might be an opportunity to get closer to one another.

I understand what it's like to come out to a family member and be met with disbelief, anger, and disappointment. It's devastating. It can disorient the way you view the world and relate to others. And if your family members apologize or otherwise come around, it's a long and exhausting journey to trust them again. You should be able to date and fall in love without worrying that your relationship with your father is irreparably changed. Sometimes our biological families fail us. You already know that, but another amazing thing about being queer is that you can build your own family. ♥

All my life, I've written off my sexuality as "not a big deal" because I was fortunate enough to be raised in a liberal and supportive environment. I'm now realizing that I have a lot of internalized homophobia and am self-sabotaging to avoid coming to terms with the reality of being gay. I almost never message girls on apps; if I do, I ghost. My college is super gay (so is the surrounding area), but I take every conversational opportunity that presents itself to say something disparaging about the gays on campus. I'm not out to my family because I don't like being vulnerable and I know they would be mushy. I hooked up with a guy when the opportunity presented itself because I was tired of feeling pathetic and inexperienced. How do I reconcile my internal fears and monologues so that I can live the lesbian life of my dreams?

—HARRIET, 18

A. Instead of disparaging the gays on campus, try spending some time with them. As they say, "If you can't beat 'em, join 'em." The lesbian life of your dreams begins with meeting some living, breathing lesbians who will show you new ways to live and relate to your queerness. You might even find a girlfriend.

I understand why you're hesitant to tell your family. You sound like someone who likes their privacy. Coming out is like telling your parents that you're having sex, or at least interested in having sex. Most people, including me, would rather not talk about sex with their parents. Straight people don't have this problem because their sex lives are the default. When you've kept something to yourself for so long, the last thing you want is a big, over-the-top reaction. But at the same time, you're not allowing your family to know the full you. You might be surprised too by how relieved you feel when you can talk openly with your parents about your life. The less you treat your lesbian-ness like a big, painful secret, the less it will actually *be* a big, painful secret. ♥

Q **Hello, I'm a lesbian** and have been out for many, many years, but ever since I realized I am also nonbinary a few years ago, I have been feeling so damn confused as to how my gender identity, which I really don't feel is *woman* the way other lesbians strongly and proudly identify with that term, can coexist with my sexuality, which is VERY MUCH being into gay women/wlw exclusively, and I just really want to know how other nonbinary dykes relate to their essentially oxymoronic gender identities and sexualities? I've seen some lesbians saying it's "okay" to be a "woman-aligned" nonbinary person and also a lesbian. But what does that mean? Does woman-aligned mean passing as a woman? And isn't that some borderline transphobic bs? A lot of questions and a lot of gender confusion to unpack. Hope you can shed some light on this phenomenon, 'cause I know I'm not the only nb lesbo out there, but I have yet to find any clear-cut answers to these thoughts.

—M, 33

GUEST EXPERT • **TYLER FORD**

A. Hi M,

There are a lot of questions in your letter, and I'm afraid to approach all of them. Alas, I chose to respond to you, specifically, because I'm a nonbinary dyke, and I knew that attempting to answer your difficult questions would kick my ass into gear to try to better answer them for myself.

The most important (and maybe most confusing) thing I can tell you is that there are no clear-cut answers to personal identity, sexuality, or gender. Our ideas of who we are are shaped by other people and our interactions with them— our families, our friends, our partners, our communities, our idols, etc. The variety of factors that inform and shape our individual desires and personhood are not easily categorizable.

With that said, take some time to think about what your most fulfilling life would entail, without comparing yourself to others or overanalyzing your impulses. What parts of other LGBTQ+ people's stories and lives resonate with you? What are you reading, listening to, watching, experiencing that excites you or fills you with a deep sense of satisfaction? What piques your curiosity? Who do you admire? Who do you want to be friends and lovers with? Who do you want to be in relation to your lovers? Some of your responses may feel contradictory, but that doesn't necessarily mean they're incompatible, or that they negate any particular aspect of your identity.

As to how your gender and sexuality can coexist: They already do. You are you. You're doing it. You're living it. And you're not alone in that. Gender-nonconforming lesbians have been kicking ass forever, using different labels (or refraining from using them) to describe themselves throughout time. Of course, "gender-nonconforming" and "nonbinary" are not synonyms, but there's overlap and common ground to be found among the experiences of those who came before us, our elders, and our peers. When you're feeling lost or confused, remember that having a complex relationship to womanhood and/or the gender binary is par for the course for lesbians, nonbinary or not.

In trying to break down your letter, I'm wondering if your question is not, "How can my gender coexist with my sexuality?" but, "How do I concisely express who I am in a way that allows others to better understand me?" And, though I've spent almost my entire career thus far explaining trans and nonbinary identity to cis people, I'm really having trouble writing to you, because identity is messy and personal, and words are never enough. Language is a beautiful gift, but at the end of the day, we all struggle to say what we mean much of the time.

I can't tell you how to best communicate who you are, or how to uninstall the file in your brain that tells you "lesbian" and "nonbinary" are mutually exclusive categories, but I can share something I recently noticed about myself: I stopped trying to figure out how to precisely define and articulate my identity once I realized that my friends and partners never needed that from me in the first place. For all my efforts to find and relay the perfect words . . . no one cares! I spent so much time trying to pin myself down, I forgot that the best feeling in the world is being present with the people I love and letting my gut guide the way.

So, you're doing fine. You don't need a lesbian stamp of approval to live your life and define yourself on your own terms—just read or reread *Stone Butch Blues*, do what you love, and go about your day. ♥

Wishing you all the best,

—TYLER FORD
Editor, Advocate & Guest Expert

THERE ARE NO SHORTCUTS

TOUGH CONVERSATIONS

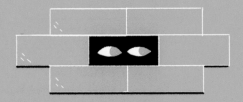

CHAPTER SIX

Kelsey and I spent a long time deciding what questions to include in this chapter. Each and every question submitted to this book could technically be categorized as a tough conversation—queer people from around the world asked us for advice on breaking up with their girlfriends, confronting a friend's hurtful behavior, or apologizing after messing up. Many people asked for help with coming out, which is a tough conversation that never really ends. The essence of this chapter is kind of like, have you ever told a friend about an issue you're having with someone, and your friend is like, "Just tell them! Tell them exactly what you told me." You know your friend is right, you need to bite the bullet and just talk to your girlfriend or coworker or whoever is causing you grief. But it's never the right time. Words fail you. Maybe things improve on their own and you decide to just let it go.

The queers in this chapter are afraid of rejection. They're afraid of being judged or dismissed. They're afraid of dredging up painful things from the past or losing a future with someone they love. All of these fears are valid. As queer women and people of marginalized genders, we're taught from infancy to hold back and censor ourselves. We worry about sounding crazy or selfish, or that our needs and secrets will be met with eye rolls and skepticism.

If you've ever kept a secret or stayed in a bad relationship because you were afraid of disappointing your partner, you know that silence is not the easy option. Even our bodies know when we're lying or denying important parts of ourselves. Our guts twist into knots. Our hearts race. Certain topics and words make us feel waves of hot and cold. It's unfair not to give someone the chance to correct their behavior, or to know you completely. It assumes that nobody is capable of hearing criticism or making a change.

There are no shortcuts for a difficult conversation. It's our official position that saying something over text or email is better than not saying it at all. Ask yourself, *Why am I struggling to speak freely? Am I feeling ashamed right now, or is there something about this relationship that's preventing me from being honest?* Tough conversations are a part of every relationship, especially your relationship with yourself.

Q.

I've done a bad thing! I met a girl on Tinder when I was in a city for a short time. We hit it off and hooked up a few times, and she made me feel good but never actually come. But it was all short-term so I did a bad, bad hetero thing and faked it. Now I've totally caught feels, we're in a relationship, and I literally have no idea what to do. I'm really turned on by her, initiate and want to have sex with her a lot, the buildup is amazing, but I've left it too long now?! We talk about sex, I show her how I like it, and we give each other good directions but still, nuh. Help.

—CLO, 33

A. A while back, I found myself longing for a real, adult relationship. I was tired of going over to someone's house to hang out and watch Netflix. I wanted to go on a real date. And then, miracle of miracles, I met someone who was all about real dates. For a month or so, it was blissful. We went to museums and botanical gardens and Thai restaurants. We had picnics on the beach and even took a weekend trip together. But the sex was hasty and awkward. Our bodies just didn't connect. Have you ever smashed teeth with someone? Have you ever smashed teeth with someone two times in a row? It's not hot. I tried to communicate, but nothing seemed to change. I felt frustrated, like I was repeating myself, or expressing things that I thought (perhaps unfairly)

should have been obvious. I spent a lot of time Googling phrases like "good relationship bad sex" or "how to make sex better." And all the advice I found were things that I, a lesbian, already knew: Good sex requires communication and asking for what you want. And also, sometimes sex is just okay and that's normal. I lost faith, Clo. I stopped caring.

In the same way that not everyone you date will understand your jokes or know the perfect thing to say when you're sad, I think that sometimes the sex chemistry just isn't there. It's your call, of course, but maybe it's time to admit that it's just not going to work. ♥

Q.

So I've been dating my current gf for about a year and I love her so much and my heart is full and all that. It's just that we never have sex anymore? Whenever I talk to her about it she says she is tired all the time (she gets up at 6 a.m. for work), which I completely understand . . . I just can't help but wonder why. It seems like we always had sex at the beginning of our relationship, and now it's just like never or I have to pretty much beg. I respect her boundaries, but I feel like I'm a pretty sexual person and I need it. I also want to explore an open relationship or maybe even group sex, and she is completely opposed to the idea. We did have a bad incident with an attempted threesome with my ex-best friend, and I don't know if that's why or if she really just isn't interested in that sort of thing, but I am and I think it would be fun. Whenever I bring it up she gets really sad and shuts down and won't talk to me about it. I just don't know what to do anymore. I know she is my person. Should I just give up on these feelings, or idk?

—SYMONE, 21

A. The situation you're describing is concerning. You should never feel like you're begging your girlfriend for sex, or like you're trying to change her mind. No matter how important sex is to you, you're not entitled to it. You don't "need" to have it. When you ask your girlfriend for a threesome and she says no, you don't get to ask again and hope for a different answer. When she shuts down and refuses to talk, that also counts as no. No means no means no times infinity.

There's so, so much advice out there about how to bring sex back into a long-term relationship. The internet is overflowing with tips like "buy some sex dice" or "kiss your partner every day and schedule time to be intimate." But all of this advice hinges on you and your girlfriend working together and wanting similar things for the future of your relationship. You cannot save the relationship by yourself; your girlfriend also has to be invested.

I have so many questions about the attempted threesome. Was it just a weird, awkward experience or was it more unsettling? Did you and your girlfriend ever discuss what happened? Is it why you and your best friend are no longer bffs?

When you love someone, it can be difficult to admit that you're not a positive presence in their life. With some serious introspection, you can grow and learn from this experience. ♥

Let me start off by saying, yes, I am a Capricorn. My girlfriend and I have been together for four and a half years and living together for three. She works as a freelancer so her finances are always wildly different month to month and she pays an enormous amount in student loans. Her loans (and money in general) give her so much anxiety that there will be days it is debilitating for her. I've been paying her portion of the rent since we moved in together three years ago, originally as a way to ease her stress about quitting her full-time job around the same time we moved in together. I also do all of the grocery shopping and am the only one to buy gas (she doesn't drive), along with handling the majority of the day-to-day expenses. I know that me doing this for her has definitely improved her situation, and she would be in a much darker place if I wasn't contributing, but three years is a long time.

I would hate, hate, hate for money to be a huge issue in our relationship, which is why I would rather just handle it, but I work in the restaurant industry and don't make enough money myself. And sometimes I can't help but feel the resentment creeping in about money. She also recently received a huge cash inheritance from one of her family member's deaths but never offered to help cover the rent for even one month, which would have helped me out a lot. I have tried to talk to her about it, but any mention of money and her perceived "failing" gives her so much anxiety that she shuts down and it is impossible to discuss it. I hate that this happens, but sometimes when we have a fight, I let the resentment about the money situation (that I usually repress) slip out and use it against her and it never goes over well. How can I approach the situation in a way that doesn't make her immediately shut down, but also gives me some kind of satisfying result? Even when it gets brought up and she says "I'll work on it, I'll get better," nothing ever changes and I feel like I can't bring it up again. I would rather use my money to buy us a house, but it's impossible to save at this point. Short of going to couples therapy, are there any other ways to navigate this problem?

A. When you initially agreed to pay your girlfriend's share of the rent, it was with the understanding that she would start contributing once the freelance checks started rolling in. You never agreed to indefinitely pay for her rent, groceries, gas, and other daily expenses. It's unfair for her to accept money that you never consented to give. However, it's also unfair for you to offer a level of support that you know is unsustainable and then lash out when you inevitably feel depleted.

From your question, it sounds like you think it's crass or immature to react emotionally to money. That's noble of you, but you're ignoring the basic fact that money is one of the most painful and emotionally charged topics on the planet. Under capitalism, money dictates whether or not we can eat when we're hungry, rest when we're tired, and access medicine when we're sick. It's a rare person who believes they will always have enough, who sees money as a free-flowing and renewable resource. Most of us live with financial uncertainty, though of course the extent varies; some people worry they'll never be able to have kids or retire, while others cannot imagine their financial situations in a week—let alone years and years out. Personally, I worry a lot about affording my therapist. I also have this very specific anxiety dream where I get in a car accident and my parents lose their house trying pay my medical bills. What I'm trying to say is that money is a big deal. When we use our money to buoy or sustain someone else, it's a significant act. It carries a lot of weight.

I also want to point out that your girlfriend, the person you share a home and finances with, has an extremely emotional relationship to money. She received an inheritance and didn't offer to cover rent, not even her own half, for a single month. That's alarming in and of itself, but it's even more alarming that you couldn't say, "Hey, can you cover rent this month? I'm struggling right now and you just got this big windfall."

The harsh, ungenerous side of me wants to know why your girlfriend, with all of her money anxiety, quit her full-time job. Like your girlfriend, I'm self-employed and have student loan debt. I love working from home and making elaborate fried egg sandwiches for lunch, but sometimes it's like, *Um, when am I getting paid?* When there's no work on the horizon, what could be a week off becomes an empty, anxiety-ridden stretch of compulsively refreshing my inbox and feeling guilty about buying coffee. But this is what

it means to live in the world, right? We all have to cope with a certain level of uncertainty and potential doom. It's when our anxiety and fears remove us from the present moment, when we're unable to show up for our relationships because we're so consumed by the unknown—that's when we need to ground ourselves in the present, and possibly seek therapy.

This brings me to my next point: Sometimes when someone we love is struggling, we forget that we're allowed to tell them no. You're allowed to save for a house. You're allowed to want a more balanced financial arrangement. What would it look like for you to accept that your girlfriend is the only one who can deal with her anxiety, fear of failure, and scarcity mindset?

I know you think you're doing your girlfriend a favor, but it's clear that neither of you is happy with the way things are. What would it look like for you to let go of the responsibility of supporting her? What would it look like for your girlfriend to respect your boundaries and work toward a more grounded relationship to money, even if it means returning to a full-time job with a steady paycheck? What would it look like to have a really honest, reciprocal discussion with each other? Three years is a long time to not be on the same page about money. Like I said, money is *emotional.* ♥

Q. My partner and I have been together for over three years. We're both in our early twenties. We seem to have hit a dry spell in our relationship; we don't have as much sex as we used to. We are either very tired or very busy. I'm wondering if I could get any advice on how to bring up opening up our relationship?

—WHITNEY, 24

A. If you and your partner feel detached and distant from each other, it might not be the best idea to bring new people and relationships into your orbit. An open relationship is not a magical reset or a chill alternative to breaking up. It's a lot of work. Your relationship needs to be in a really, really solid place. Your communication and boundary-setting need to be Olympic-level good. Most of all, you both need to be excited

about opening up your relationship. You have to share a vision.

Have you and your partner ever talked about an open relationship, even in the abstract? If this is totally new, be prepared for your partner to feel hurt or confused. There isn't some special way you need to spin it, just be honest about what you're envisioning. There's a lot to discuss, so take your time. Read a book like *Redefining Our Relationships* by Wendy-O Matik. Some questions to ask each other: Are you prepared if one of you starts seeing other people first? If you live together, is it okay to bring

dates back to your shared space? What amount of information will you share with each other about your other partners and relationships? Will you describe each other as primary partners or do you not want any kind of hierarchy? How do you each experience jealousy?

I don't mean to sound discouraging, but I am a pragmatic midwestern lesbian. I hope you know that I'm rooting for you, and your partner, and all the tired, busy queers out there. ♥

My partner, G, and I have been together for five years, and are very much in love. They are four years older than I am and have been pressuring me hard to think about starting a family and building a little nest. Baby fever big time. The thing is, I don't have it . . . yet. I'm still recovering from traumatic events and abuse in my childhood and very much still feel like I'm crossing experiences off my list, experiences that most twentysomethings have earlier in life. I don't know what awaits us in the future, because I think G feels duped by my constant reply of "maybe in the next five years." But that never changes, even though years keep going by. How do I figure out what I want and hang on to a relationship that we've both fought hard to make healthy and good?

—R, 28

A. You're afraid of disappointing G and losing the relationship altogether. Unfortunately, there's no great compromise when it comes to something as momentous and life-defining as parenthood. You can't meet each other in the middle and, like, get a dog. You say G is pressuring you—do you mean they're looking for a clear answer? Or is there not space for you to say no or share your apprehensions? While G should respect your uncertainty, it sounds like they've always been forthcoming and open about their desire to become a parent. And to be fair, G's impatience and anxiety isn't unfounded—there are many paths to queer parenthood, but almost all of them require intention and determination. A baby will not happen overnight or even in a year. The only certainty is that it will be very, very expensive. It's not something G can do alone and still consider you their partner.

How do you figure out if you want to become a parent?

There's no set of instructions for this. Instead of agonizing over whether or not you'll feel ready for a baby in the future, focus on what you know at this moment: You need time to heal from your own childhood, there's still so much you want to do before becoming a parent, and you just don't feel ready yet. Hold this self-knowledge close. It's sacred.

The most difficult part of any relationship is figuring out what you owe yourself and what you owe the other person. You don't owe G a baby—not now, not ever. You do, however, owe them a more direct and honest answer than "maybe in the next five years." ♥

 My best friend dated only men until she met the love of her life, a woman, and got married. I have been an out bisexual woman for years but am currently dating a man. Recently she has started to make some comments about her "always being gay" and that males are "trash" and so forth. I know she is just processing, but it hurts as it seems like she judges and thinks less of me, and it feels like she doesn't want to use the word "bisexual" for herself. Am I being stupid? Can I approach her about it without hurting anyone? Should I let her go through her "the only lesbian is a gold star and the men I've had don't count" phase and just come out on the other side, or do I have a bisexual duty to inform her?

—KESHA, 25

A. Your friend exclusively dated men before finding a sense of home in lesbian identity. From your perspective, it seems obvious that she's actually bisexual. However, it's not at all unusual for people to identify as straight or bisexual before arriving at lesbian. Some people's sexualities shift and change over time. You can't tell your friend how to identify. It's not for you to say.

The real issue is that your friend is making comments that feel directed at you in a very specific, sneaky way. It's possible your friend is just oblivious and venting about men,

or maybe she feels insecure or like a "bad lesbian," and your confident, flagrant bisexuality feels like an affront. One thing that's for certain is that you're brushing up against each other in uncomfortable, hurtful ways. The sign of a solid, caring friendship is being able to discuss your feelings. Say something like, "Sometimes I feel like you're judging me or tearing me down. I'd like to talk about it directly, so that there are no misunderstandings." This way your friend has an opportunity to reconsider her words, and you're not stewing in anger and assuming the worst. ♥

Howdy! About a year ago I left an emotionally abusive relationship and moved across the country to heal, apply to graduate programs, and be closer to my family. All has gone pretty well since then, minus the average human tragedies. I got into grad school, am with someone new and wonderful, feel like myself again—but the relationship I left still haunts me. Mostly because pretty much no one in the circle we were in knew or knows what happened. I didn't feel like it was right to share it with that group since my ex was still very embedded there. I felt like they weren't a repeat offender, so to speak, and I was scared of talking about it. I think I regret that now, since it's been a year and I have unresolved feelings I don't know what to do with. That relationship really did a number on me for the year or so when things got bad, and now I see them involved in the scene, see their name, and it makes me a little upset to continue to see their presence on my friends' feeds. I don't think there's a way to talk about it now to the people they're still involved with who count me as a friend, and even making art about it makes me nervous—anyone might see what I've made and have questions about it. Is there a way to make peace with this thing that happened, to speak about it without feeling guilty? I am not sure how to approach it. Is the best thing now to just try to let it go as much as possible? I'm not sure how to do that.

—LORENA, 24

A. When I was nineteen, I was in a relationship with a manipulative and controlling person. She would pour on love and affection one day, then completely ignore me for a week. I had just come out to myself, my family, and the larger world, and she was constantly finding ways to tell me that without her, my queerness was just a phase. She isolated me from my friends and eroded my confidence in innumerable, insidious ways. My first year after the breakup was like swimming away from a shipwreck or purging my body from poison. I struggled to describe the relationship to my friends, many of whom were also close with my ex. When I finally found the language of emotional abuse, I confided in my best friend. She was supportive and shared her own observations of our relationship—she had sensed things were unbalanced and off but didn't say anything for fear of overstepping. I felt an indescribable sense of relief. Finally, someone understood that I was experiencing something beyond normal breakup sadness and angst. After our conversation, my best friend continued to spend time with my ex. I saw their friendship on Facebook and it stung. It didn't help that when I told my other friends, they reacted with uncomfortable silence. One time, a friend came up to me drunk at a party and told me I was just being dramatic. I felt completely gutted. I knew what I had experienced, but nobody else seemed to care.

Almost ten years later, time has scrubbed my ex from my life completely. I'm not sure I would recognize her in public. Even so, when I sat down to write this response, I felt the shame and hesitation you're describing. I worried that she would read this and find a way to punish or contact me. And this is the really shitty thing about abuse, right? It plants a chip in your brain that expects retaliation and conflict.

I imagine that like a lot of abuse, what you experienced happened in private. You were probably hiding the truth from your friends and yourself. On

top of everything, your ex likely said and did things that made you doubt your own feelings and perceptions. When you see your friends uplifting and supporting them via social media, it feels like proof that you imagined the abuse. When really, abusive people are often strategic and selective with their tactics. They don't want to get caught and lose access to their community, so they project an image of themselves as caring and kind. To most people, your ex probably seems like a nice, regular person. I know how disturbing a realization this can be. It's enraging and unfair. Please believe me when I say that no matter how many people your ex has duped, your experiences and pain are still valid.

Right now, you want to find a place for your anger and confusion. You don't want to live your life on silent mode anymore. If you feel pulled to make art, you should. You don't have to show anyone else or offer any explanation. When I'm writing about something that feels scary or painful to me, I keep it low stakes—I journal on scrap paper or open an iPhone note. Translating some of your feelings into art will help you envision a path forward or allow you to create a record of your healing process. Try to connect with people who will validate your experiences,

whether that's through joining a support group, talking to a trustworthy friend, or reading a topical book like Carmen Maria Machado's *In the Dream House*.

My biggest advice is to be patient with yourself—a year is not a long time to recover from a breakup, especially when abuse has ripped through your heart and self-esteem like a tornado. A while back, I was in a healthy relationship that ended in a totally amicable and mutual breakup. I was single for a year afterward, and when I met someone new, I was like, "Wait, am I really ready for another relationship? It's only been a year." You're doing amazing

work taking steps forward—you moved across the country, started grad school, and began a new relationship. You'll have days where you feel totally crushed and like right there, back with your ex, and you'll have triumphant days when you don't think about your ex at all. You'll have days where you just feel off-center and a little feral. It's never a linear path, but you will get yourself back eventually. It just takes time. ♥

Q. **I (NB, 23) am a chronically ill** wheelchair user, and I live in London, UK. I've been living here for several years now, but only became a wheelchair user a couple of years ago. When I first came to London, I had loads of friends, and dated A Lot of people, of all genders. That's how I met my current partner, who I've been with happily for four years now. In those four years, I went from having a big, active social life to having just my partner and one close friend. When my health started to decline, I became housebound for a long time due to living in inaccessible housing, and I lost nearly all my friends. Some of them just gradually stopped talking to me, but some of them made it hurt, and made it clear that me being sick (and sad about it) was both a deliberately malicious attention grab on my part and too much for them to watch. They cut all contact and took the rest of those social circles with them. Being housebound and alone was traumatizing. It took a long time to get out of that situation. With all that time alone, I was desperate to make new friends. I was sure that once I had a power chair and lived somewhere accessible (basically once I could Go Outside by myself), it would all be different: I would rebuild my support network from the ground up. Well, I've had a power chair and lived somewhere accessible for two years now, and I have very little to show for my efforts. There are two obstacles that have been stopping me from making friends. First of all, the people who hurt me while I was housebound seemingly know every gay in the city, and I don't really want to be within their circle of influence. I know they've continued to spread rumors about me since then—one of the people from that group even tried to persuade my caregiver at a party to stop working for me! The second barrier has been how ableist the entire London LGBT scene is. If a venue is even accessible in the first place, no one wants to be the one talking to a wheelchair user—unless they're looking for Good Person Points. There have been times when I've gone to social events and there's been a five-foot bubble of space around me; they were that keen to avoid me. I wouldn't want to be friends with people who behave like that, but the problem is that it seems to be 99 percent of LGBT people in this city who are like that, and the 1 percent is mostly other physically disabled people. It's not easy being friends with them either, because public spaces are only designed for one mobility aid at a time. So, these are my questions: How do I cope with existing in the same city as people who have hurt me and continue to demonstrate that they wish me future harm? How do I cope with sharing social circles with them? How do I deal with friends who struggle with being around me when I never miraculously stop being chronically ill? How can I break the ice with LGBT people who've never spoken to a wheelchair user before? Apps are only good if people will read past the sentence "I'm disabled" without swiping away . . . Sorry this one got so long!!

—L, 23

GUEST EXPERT • **KALYN ROSE HEFFERNAN**

A. Greetings from Denver, Colorado, all the way across the pond!

First of all, way to fricken go! Way to navigate your new sexy body in such a short amount of time. Way to be vulnerable and bold enough to share your experience and ask the questions that you have. Hurray for your accessible housing and power chair and all the support systems you've had to build and maintain, including your partnership!! This shit ain't easy— and it can take decades to do what you've done in just a few years. You did dat!

My life experience is obviously way different from yours—I'm about ten years older than you, I was born with my disability, and I got my first power chair when I was a toddler. Somehow, I have always collected a circus of people around me (for the better and worse), and I'm small enough to be carried up and down this inaccessible world. I can still relate on a lot of levels though, especially on the relationships part!

Relationships are suuuuuuch a labor of love. To me, they're life's most valuable asset. They're so beautifully messy and take a ton of work to maintain. They can be draining, and they can be the most energizing feeling in the world. They change, they grow, they move, they hurt, they die, they shift, and yet, at least for me . . . they never ever stop feeling. There is nothing more rewarding than a healthy, balanced, mutual friendship that encourages each other's healing. But you know, since we're humans and holding on to all this trauma, everything's got to be complicated as hell—not to mention nothing is forever and the world is on fire. So we break up with friends and lovers and then have to refind ourselves and our communities all over again.

Relationships push us to uncover the most beautiful and most agonizing parts of ourselves.

Love and trust force us to communicate through our most vulnerable moments. Relationships push us to limits we didn't know we had until they were tested and sometimes crossed. This ableist world makes our existence even more vulnerable and reliant on support. As disabled queers, we really rely on community care and embody the beautiful importance of interdependence. We are surviving in these challenging bodies inside this haggard system that's been working day in and day out for centuries to keep us from living our best lives . . . and hell!!! LIFE IS A LOT!

But you, dear, are killing it. You're growing, and finding new purpose and better reasons to make yourself happy. You are so much bigger than that small queer circle you're dearly departing, and London is waaaay bigger than all of you. I just looked it up and cannot believe how many of you there are! There are most certainly some queers craving the same type of community you're waiting for, and there HAVE to be some queers out there who are making it happen.

You have plenty of time to find your squad, and the goal is to never stop curating the best collective you can. It's clear those queers you speak of aren't a part of that crew, or at least not right now. Maybe they were at a time, but you've changed, and maybe you have higher standards for your circle now, which is dope! Maybe those spots aren't as cool as they were a few years ago. Remember, we're not all at the same place on this spiritual journey spectacle, and there's always room to grow. Those people may not be ready to accept such a fabulous body as yours, and shoot . . . you may not have been either until you had to. That does NOT mean it is your responsibility to hold their hands through the awkwardness, or be the one to "expose" them to disability, or wait around for them to catch up. Your responsibility is to be your best self with your best tools so you can adapt to all the changes to come.

My favorite quote ever, which gets me every time, is: "All that you touch You Change. All that you Change Changes you. The only lasting truth is Change. God is Change." —Octavia Butler

Now that we're moving into this new decade, I've been reflecting a lot on the eras of relationships I moved through, the ones I still have, and all the changes I survived in between. I've been trying to organize these memories—big events, breakups, trips, new loves, and tragedies from the past ten years—into an analog timeline in my notebook. Partly because I hate how the internet owns so much of my life's memories, but also because everything moves faster and gets blurrier with age. It has been such a fulfilling project to honor my little life, and now I get to look back at this long page of absurdities and recognize how much I've done or how much I've survived. I super recommend trying it. Go through your social media and mark down your big accomplishments, big changes, big relationships, new cats, breakups, etc. You will see how much you've done, how many eras you've survived, and how many uncomfortable instances you moved through in the past ten years.

If you tried to tell twenty-three-year-old Kalyn (me) that I'd have the squad I have now, where I'm one of a few who even drinks anymore, I wouldn't believe you. If you told twenty-three-year-old me that I'd be known for anything other than rapping, or that I'd roll for mayor, or be a teacher, or that I'd be dating a fine-ass femme with the same disability, or begging for physical therapy, or that I would be published in a book for my opinion!? I MOST DEFINITELY wouldn't believe you!

Time is weird, relationships are wild, and space is important. Sometimes friendships are temporary and sometimes they're forever. While you have zero control over how people act, or even how you feel sometimes, you do have all the control to choose who you want to be around and who you spend your energy investing in. It sounds to me like you're already moving through an era you've outgrown.

All breakups bring us closer to the intimacy we deserve, but I'm always reminded that healing is NOT linear. Just when I think I've "moved on" from an old relationship, my past sneaks back to haunt me, inspire me, bring me back down, reconnect me, or empower me to keep working. Breakups are hard, friend breakups even harder, and in my experience band breakups are the absolute hardest. Recently, some deaths near and dear to my band have reconnected me with an old era of life and relationships. My ex is in town for the funeral, and I literally just got home from having dinner with a bandmate who I haven't seen or spoken to since we broke up at least six years ago. It just wasn't in my emotional budget until now.

One of my best friends loves to check me on emotional budgeting, and it sounds to me like the crew you're dissociating from is a bigger expense than you can afford. I'd encourage you not to give them all the power and credit for London's queer scene. You're dreaming up a different scene, a more serving group of friends, a more intersectional, socialized squad—keep doing that. Fantasize about what that looks like to you, what it feels like, and fantasize about your

dreamiest gang ever. Hell, for all you know you may have to organize to lead it someday. It's up to us to crip the future! If we can't dream up these systems, they'll never exist and neither will we. If we don't write ourselves into the future, who will?

Another quote I love so much is: "What you pay attention to grows." —adrienne maree brown (I highly recommend her books *Pleasure Activism* and *Emergent Strategy*.)

A few years ago, I was in a real sad and dark place when I recognized that I did all this activism and knew about all these movements and their historic figures, except for the disability rights movement. I began to realize I was the only wheelchair at every protest, and when anyone took the bullhorn to speak on "intersectionality," they would hardly ever mention disability. I was finally ready to confront this reality, but the only person I could really confront immediately was my damn self. I bought a few books on disability history and have had to unlearn sooo much ableism within myself ever since. Shortly after this spiral, I landed at a direct action where I joined the group ADAPT to literally sit-in in our senator's office demanding to keep our health "benefits." Actions like this were happening across the country, we made it for three days before being arrested, and it worked (for now). This one single action pushed me into such an authentic relationship with some of the disability community here in Denver, and from them, I learned that a lot of those historical figures I was craving to know about were right here doing the damn thing for the past forty-plus years. I am ashamed to say I didn't know much about ADAPT until we had that weekend rendezvous. I had no idea Denver was an epicenter for access, and I'm STILL learning about Denver's historic influence in the disability rights movement. I've been disabled my whole thirty-plus-years life, in this city for most of it, protesting since middle school, and still have so much work to do and so much to learn. I took the bus from the same corner, in front of the same intersection with a statue that marked the place where public

transportation would be forced into accessibility, for twenty years and I had NO IDEA till now.

Your frustrations, pain, and uncertainty are all valid and real, and I am confident you will push through and find yourself right where you need to be in no time. One of my biggest fears as an artist is staying stagnant. It's just too tricky for us humans to stay in the same place consistently because stability and comfort is a helluva drug. Look at all this havoc we humans have caused. If we didn't have these breaking points, how would we move to be better lovers or better protectors?

So how do you break the ice with strangers that may or may not get it? Well I think you already break ice just by being out and proud in spaces, by being active in your community. I personally am into sarcasm and grotesque humor. So I might fart right away to break the ice, but maybe that's not you. I'm the type who would make fun of the awkwardness and try to reveal it for what it is. For example, "Damn, it's like no one here has ever seen a person in a wheelchair feeling themself?" or "So, uh, you haven't talked to someone in a wheelchair before? Well, lemme be your first, my name's _____, now buy me a drink?" Or maybe take all the space you can in the middle of the dance floor with your fine self! You already are attracting attention as the only wheelchair in most of these places, so why not take the spotlight? Then again, I'm a rapper who puts myself on stage, and I realize that's not everyone's bag. People are awkward af, and I personally like to make fun of it as often as possible. People are also conditioned to think of us crips as passive, or insecure, or sheltered, so I prefer to make a scene . . . sometimes. There are also plenty of times where I just don't have the capacity or tenacity to go out, and be high-fived by all the bros, and fetishized, or applauded for just dancing on my friends. Ask yourself always, "Is it really in the budget?"

I hope some of this helps; I can't wait to hear from you in a few years, killing it. I'm not super connected to the London scene, but I hope to be someday and will keep an eye out for cute queers making radical space happen. Also, I'm just exiting my Saturn Return, which you will enter in the next few years, and oooh lemme tell you, there's so much more in store for you. So buckle up, buckaroo, you got another cosmic shift coming your way. Let these years be the perfect time to build yourself, build your support, and dream your future, and you will be way more equipped to handle what life keeps throwing your way.

So much love to you, you've done so much. Keep on keeping on! ❤

—**KALYN ROSE HEFFERNAN**
Activist, Rapper & Guest Expert

P.S. My gf just recommended these books to the both of us: *The Body Is Not an Apology: The Power of Radical Self-Love* by Sonya Renee Taylor and *Care Work: Dreaming Disability Justice* by Leah Lakshmi Piepzna-Samarasinha.

GUEST EXPERT BIOS

Ellen Kempner is a songwriter, guitarist, and singer. She's been writing and performing as Palehound since 2014, and has released three albums and one EP. Ellen loves traveling and has toured the United States and Europe extensively with inspiring artists such as Big Thief, Waxahatchee, Courtney Barnett, Speedy Ortiz, and many more. After coming out as queer on her second album, she's made it a priority to make her shows safe spaces for LGBTQA+ folks to feel free and joyous. Recently, that has included being vocal about her experience as a fat woman in rock music. Ellen is into the idea of "body neutrality" as an alternative to "body positivity." It's less condescending, and in a perfect world, our bodies and how they appear wouldn't hold as much stock as they currently do in society. Ellen lives in New York with her beautiful partner and cat.

JD Samson is best known for being part of the feminist performance project Le Tigre and as a member of the multimedia music group MEN. JD's practice has developed over the years with a specific interest in the adaptation of mediums, from film to visual art, music, writing, and performance. JD is an assistant arts professor at NYU's Clive Davis Institute of Recorded Music and has had recent collaborations with choreographer Julie Cunningham, director Sam Green, and her band, CRICKETS (with Michael O'Neill and Roddy Bottum). JD is writing a book about her failures in relationships.

Kalyn Rose Heffernan is the wheelchair-using, rapping/beat-making, activist/educator/foul-mouthed rabble-rouser who led Denver's first disabled queer artist campaign for the mayoral seat in 2019. She was born and raised in the Denver metro area, where she has been advocating for herself and other marginalized, vulnerable communities for most of her life. Kalyn fronts the internationally acclaimed band Wheelchair Sports Camp. She also teaches music production through a social justice lens with Youth on Record, using raps and beats to build trust with and futures for underserved Denver teens. A freedom fighter for the little ones, Kalyn is always on the front lines pushing and shouting for access and equity, and calling out those in power who protect capital interests—with her very distinct, high-pitched sense of humor.

Lola Pellegrino is a Brooklyn-based nurse practitioner born on the same day as Dolly Parton and Edgar Allan Poe. She was a staff writer at *Rookie Magazine* (RIP) and a frequent contributor to *The Hairpin* (RIP). She is passionate about driving very fast and the triumph of good over evil. She is @damsorrow everywhere.

Mey Rude is a fat, queer, trans Latina living in LA. She works as a daily contributor to *Out* magazine, and as a trans consultant and speaker. You might know her work from Autostraddle.com or the many queer comics she's consulted on, like *Lumberjanes*, *Stage Dreams*, and *Bitch Planet*. She loves animation, weed, and talking about her feelings.

Samantha Irby writes a blog called *bitches gotta eat*. She is the author of three books: *Meaty, We Are Never Meeting in Real Life,* and *Wow, No Thank You.*

Tyler Ford is a writer, an editor, and an award-winning nonbinary advocate. Formerly the deputy editor of Condé Nast's *them.*, Tyler has also worked as a research editor at the *New York Times* and was a grand marshal of NYC Pride 2018.

RESOURCES

COMING OUT, MENTAL HEALTH & SEXUAL VIOLENCE

PFLAG

PFLAG is a national grassroots organization that aims to support LGBTQIA+ people and their families. There are chapters across the United States that provide scholarships, family counseling, and advocacy resources. www.pflag.org

RAINN

RAINN offers free, confidential chat and phone hotlines for sexual assault survivors and their loved ones. The victim services experts at RAINN take a victim-centered, trauma-informed approach. www.rainn.org

Trans Lifeline

Trans Lifeline is a trans-led organization and phone hotline directing emotional and financial support to trans people in crisis. Their website also hosts a wellspring of legal information and resources. www.translifeline.org

The Trevor Project

The Trevor Project offers crisis intervention, suicide prevention, and mental health resources for LGBTQIA+ young people. www.thetrevorproject.org

QUEER RELATIONSHIPS & SEX

Autostraddle

Autostraddle is a lesbian and queer online community founded in 2009. It has tons of thoughtful, generous resources on coming out, disability, dating, having sex for the first time, gender expression, and queer history. Whatever questions you may have, Autostraddle probably has an answer. *www.autostraddle.com*

Nancy Podcast

Nancy is a podcast hosted by Kathy Tu and Tobin Low. Although the final episode aired in 2020, the *Nancy* archive is a wonderful, diverse compendium of queer communities and experiences. *www.wnycstudios.org/podcasts/nancy*

Scarleteen: Sex Ed for the Real World

Scarleteen is an inclusive, feminist resource about relationships and sexual health. The site is aimed at teens and young adults, but it's extremely useful for people of all ages. *www.scarleteen.com*

LOCAL & IRL RESOURCES

If you live in a midsize to large city, it's likely there's an LGBTQIA+ neighborhood, health clinic, and community center near you. If you live in a small town, there may be a PFLAG chapter. Small, independent bookstores are also a good place to find queer books and resources.

ACKNOWLEDGMENTS

Every book is a collaboration and *Ex-Girlfriend* is no exception. Kelsey and I owe a debt of gratitude to many, many people. To everyone who submitted a question: This book would not exist without your vulnerability and openness. Thank you. And thank you so, so much to our guest contributors: Ellen Kempner, JD Samson, Kalyn Rose Heffernan, Lola Pellegrino, Mey Rude, Samantha Irby, and Tyler Ford. We would also like to thank all of the people who ordered, shared, and evangelized the *Ex-Girlfriend* zines. You are the true force behind this book. And to the USPS postal workers who helped the zines travel and find new homes around the world—thank you, thank you, thank you. You deserve a raise and everything good in life.

We would also like to thank Natalie Butterfield, our editor at Chronicle Books, who saw potential in this project from the very beginning. We're indebted to Ed Maxwell, our agent, who graciously stepped in sporting his signature bowtie to help us navigate the business side of things. We are also grateful to Lizzie Vaughan, the designer who made this book look amazing. And of course, big gratitude to Anna Svoboda-Stel, who introduced us and suggested we make a book together. Midwestern lesbians assemble!

And finally, to Kelsey's partner, Allyson, for always being her #1 fan, and Maddy's mom, Sandra, for always showing up with snacks.